Are You Sure You Want to Go Back to College?

Survival Guide for Students Over 30

Sabrina Hartel

DEDICATION

To my ex-husband Mark who supported my efforts
of going back to college over 30

CONTENTS

Introduction   7

1 Preparing to Step in It   Pg 8

2 Stuff You'll Need to Know Before You Register   Pg 14

3 Scheduling: Yes, You Actually Have to Show Up!   Pg 27

4 How in the World Are You Going to Pay for This?   Pg 30

5 What Will You Wear?   Pg 39

6 Major Pains: Choosing Your Classes   Pg 43

7 What Happens Now?   Pg 55

8 The Coursework Situation   Pg 61

9 The 15 Commandments of Classroom Etiquette   Pg 80

10 Don't Panic! Okay, Maybe a little   Pg 85

11 Graduation: Are You Still Alive?   Pg 97

12 The [Dreadful] Workplace   Pg 101

13 Advice from Nontraditional Students   Pg 119

INTRODUCTION

Maybe you're stuck in a dead-end job, or maybe you feel like you've made the wrong career choice. Or just maybe, stepping into the role of *Holly Homebody* or *Father Knows Best* didn't peg the 401k-plan results you had anticipated. You were probably in your 20s when you made that decision. Who doesn't make bad choices then? The good news is that it's not too late to go back to college. The bad news is, your brain has probably been withering at the academic wayside.

But going back to college as an older student definitely has its perks: You have a lot experience setting priorities; your attention span is longer than a Warble Fly; and you're there because you want to be—not because you saw an opportunity to flee your parent's home, though getting away from your current boss or spouse is another predicament altogether.

This book will demystify your social and academic concerns about returning to college as a mature, undergraduate student. Because knowledge is power. Albeit, it may also make you swing a u-turn and run for the nearest border. College is not the place it was when you left it, perhaps 10 or 20 years ago. It certainly wasn't for me when I re-enlisted at 32 years old as a freshman. The place was a jungle gym. I wasn't prepared for the academic-life pitfalls and socialization amongst a mob of early 20-somethings. You shall not share the same fate.

1 PREPARRING TO STEP INTO IT

ARE YOU SURE YOU WANT TO GO BACK TO COLLEGE?

Some jobs don't require a college degree like a full-time stay-at-home parent, an artist, actor, writer, juggler, bus driver, police officer, real estate broker, construction worker or sales representative. If you'd like to make one of these your profession then you're off the hook. If not, you've got work to do, like thinking of going back to college.

The first thing you must do is let your partner or spouse in on your proposed conquest. Scenario one response: "Honey, we need you here—me and the kids and the dog and the chores."—you crawl back into your hole. Scenario two: "Great! I'm glad you decided to take up a hobby."… In that case, most likely, he or she will become the stranger who sleeps in your bedroom when your professors decide to let you come home. If you don't have a partner or spouse, then you must let yourself in on the idea that you're actually going back to school. Then you've got to decide if college is something you can do outside of your head.

College is an emotional and financial investment, not a feat that's done between chores. College will consume your life. College will be your life for the next few months or years, although towards the end, you'd wish it would all just go away. The last thing you'd want to do is bog down your loved ones with Macbeth tragedies and Socrates' rants. When I was failing algebra, which

I so humblingly divulge in my memoir *"Setting My Apron on Fire: Housewife Turned Undergraduate Student,"* I had night terrors, spotting my professor plodding through weeded fields like Big Foot. Now that I've talked most of you out of it, are the rest of you still with me? Good!

*** The average age of a community college student is 29.[i] ***

It's best to have a clear idea of your goals and why college might be right for you. This way you can better prepare yourself for the challenges ahead, because there will be challenges. Scramble through your brain and make a list. Is it that you want to make more money? A career switch? Could it be that your job industry is downsizing, sending jobs overseas and you've been perspiring ever since? Is it for self-esteem reasons or just something you've always wanted to do? Having a solid plan will keep you focused on the end and not the journey.

CHOOSING A COLLEGE OR UNIVERSITY

Research colleges before you step right in. Universities can be a strange place, despite what the admissions' clerk tells you over the phone. Narrow your results to at least three choices and kick the tires. Look under the hood. Interview the school. A college is a business, so don't fall privy to the four-color-process marketing brochure. You know the one with the sun-beamy students resting on the freshly mowed lawn? Caveat emptor to truth in advertising, ye sovereign thou. The photographer sweetened the deal with headshots on the side, so ask the students, in person, how they feel about doing time there. Go on Facebook and "like" the college, then snoop to see what kind of feedback they get. They won't be shy in their responses. They'll sing like shiny superstars on American Idol.

If you live in an urban area, you're in good hands. And not with Allstate. Most

9

cities have city colleges, which means lower tuition and an easier commute. A dorm-room situation is obviously not going to work. Just because a college has "city" or "state" in the name doesn't mean it is a city or state run institution. You can also choose a private college or university. Perhaps your friends or family members are alumni. Perhaps you've always wanted to join the exclusive football team to become a cheerleader or linebacker. Perhaps the university is three blocks away from your home. Whatever your reasons, watch out for your class credits if you transfer from a two-year college, to a four-year college or university. Some of your transfer credits may end up in the trash bin because the course doesn't exist at the transfer college, or the class doesn't equal to the current class's curriculum. Plus, if your grades aren't what they used to be, a parent college is more forgiving with a "D" grade to their current students than they are to outsiders.

A maximum number of credits are transferable too. Coming from a two-year college, most schools will only accept about 60 credits. That's equivalent to two years of schooling. If your parent college is a four-year institution, they may accept more, but you'd still have to take a minimum number of credits at the transfer college to graduate, somewhere in the neighborhood of 30 credits. This will take a lot of fore planning, as in knowing which college you want to go to and getting someone on the phone to ask about those credits if you plan to transfer. Sticking to one college is better than shifting to another one later.

Also, make sure the college or university is accredited. Accreditation gives the school certification—making sure they are up to standards—with courses that are nationally recognized and mostly accepted. These schools are regularly scrutinized for quality control, so don't be shy to ask if you're not sure.

COURSE PLACEMENT

Failing all or part of entrance exams will score you for remedial courses at some colleges and some colleges might not accept you. Don't frat because it's not unusual to have to start at the bottom. In fact, according to College Board, 77 percent of students take math as a remedial course, with writing trailing at 35 percent. These classes fill up fast, not to mention it's where the entire freshman class hangs out. Think of these as "refresh-man" courses if you find yourself in this situation.

The National Center for Education Statistics has implemented this nifty little widget to search for colleges in the U.S. by location, criteria and program majors: http://nces.ed.gov/ipeds/cool/

Some colleges have G.E.D. classes if you don't have a high school diploma. You can even take some college courses while you're going over the rudiments of high school history and science. I don't think they'll have you dissecting toads, but I'd surely look into it if you have a reptilian phobia.

THE MESS YOU'LL LEAVE BEHIND

Who's going to watch the kids? You'll need a babysitter to watch the children while you study. And no, you can't get your homework done while Lil' Johnny is trying to illustrate his new potty-training technique—or lure an aquatic insect into Susie's bedroom. Some courses demand your full attention, such as analyzing the infancy of the woman's movement with Lucy Stone, or John Wayne's character influence on male masculinity.

You simply won't have time to pull your weight around the castle. Suppose your duty is to take out the trash, the garbage area will look as though a herd of rat-packin', mother-in-laws rifled through it. The professor's ego wouldn't accept anything less than consuming your weekdays, weekends and holidays too! Maximizing your time is of essence. Let your neighbors know that you're going back to college, so they can purge the Saturday afternoon fiestas, because that term paper will wait for no one.

POINTS TO REMEMBER

- Have a clear idea of why you want to go back to college, so you can keep your eyes on the prize to get you through. Things will get testy.

- College is an emotional and financial investment, so get the family involved because your decisions will affect them.

- Don't get swayed by the college's marketing department with fancy brochures. A college is still a business. Go for quality, not for a college's stellar football team, although you might get teased if they truly eat dirt.

- No one has a patent on the words "city" or "state." A public or private college can use either one of these terms and charge as much tuition as they'd like. And you can pick which one you'd like to go to.

- Accreditation of a college means you can take your credits all over the United States. Plus, the college has met the standard requirements of what a school should model.

2 STUFF YOU'LL NEED BEFORE YOUR REGISTER

BEFORE YOU GO

SIGNING UP

You've probably been out of school since Neil Armstrong gallivanted across the moon. But yes, the college still wants your previous high school and college transcripts, and your SAT's and ACT's. The administrators want to measure your scholastic intellect. Though in recent years, the SAT has been getting a bad rap. Social Scientist Charles Murray (who wrote the book, *Losing Ground* and *The Bell Curve*, co-written with Richard J. Herrnstein) proposed that the SAT be eliminated altogether because the test favors privilege individuals. In essence, privilege kids are smart because their parents are smart.[ii] But right now, some colleges still want them.

Send for these items at least three months in advance, five months if you've been out of school for more than 20 years. Since, they've computerized their files, but your original, paper version is probability in the basement collecting cobwebs.

Don't worry too much about the acronymed exams if you have been to college before, especially to get into a city or state college. But a private college or university might give you misery for the lack of SAT paraphernalia. Be aware that SAT's and ACT's have expiration dates too. So if it's been a while since you've been in the game, don't be surprised if you have to take them again.

You may also have to write a personal statement, an essay about yourself and your goals. This is like a sale's pitch, so make it relevant and be sincere. In most cases, you can talk about your return to college as an older student, though be sure to tie that in to the question at hand if any. Stay away from controversial topics too. And you want this piece of work in the best shape possible. So have your spouse, a librarian, or even your kids to look it over once you've completed it.

PROOF OF RESIDENCY

Colleges have this thing about residency, living within their stumping ground. The tuition is up to 100 percent more for non-natives of the municipality. Out-of-state students are flipped upside down then rattled until lint falls from both pockets. But why stop there? Even supposing you move to the new state, you have to prove residency for at least one year. Make sure your driver's license matches your (in-state) address and keep those old telephone bills, a sweet reminder of how cheap talking to Aunt Beatrice used to be.

UP TO DATE WITH YOUR IMMUNIZATIONS?

Most colleges or universities require proof of vaccinations, so have your medical records ready. College kids are contagious! Well, people gathered in such small quarters are suspect, apparently, according to the Department of Education. In all likelihood, you've had the pleasure of needle pricks before you started kindergarten in the United States. If you haven't, it's time to get over your needle phobia and head down to the Department of Public Health and roll up your sleeves. They'll give you "school shots" free. If you've lost your immunization records, you'd have to get your Measles, Mumps and Rubella (MMR) shots repeated. The lady at the Health Department assured me that I wasn't going to die of Toxic Shock when I had a do-over. My childhood vaccination records were six states over and 20 years in the past. It wasn't worth it to me to start that kind of adventure.

Persons with pre-existing conditions should consult a doctor before getting vaccinated, especially a second time around. Also, some schools may want you to get an optional Meningitis vaccine. If you have a dorm-room situation, they will *make* you get it. That is, if you want to live in the dorms.

PRIVACY CONCERNS

You'll have to give up your social security number if you decided to go back to college. All those years your parents taught you to guard that "serial number" with your life. Identity theft hasn't made you sleep easier either. Crooks are on the loose with credit card scams. They're even becoming dead people (at their own peril!). But the college wants this number so they can keep track of you. They'll call it your "student I.D. number." However, in most cases, you can opt out and use a different identification number. But if you're receiving federal student aid or attending a college or university that does receive federal funds, you might have to give it up for tax purposes and identification.

SOME DEGREES COST MORE THAN OTHERS

Some degrees cost more than others at public universities. A business degree, for example, cost $500 more each semester at the University of Wisconsin. And at the University of Nebraska, engineering students pay $40 more per credit hour, roughly $120 more per class. Journalism students? Get ready to pay $250 more per semester at Arizona State University—even though a journalist's salary isn't stellar. The reasons stated behind this extortion effort are that public universities need to hire quality professors, like their private cohorts.[iii]

Private universities haven't caught on to this trend. Then again, their tuition is higher overall. I don't doubt for a second that they'd turn down this lucrative opportunity to put more money into their pocketbooks when they get a chance.

MYTHS ABOUT COLLEGE

Several myths exist about college, though some are rarely true. Surely you have some sloshing in your brain right now. Round 'em up and stick them into the attic. Let's separate truth from myth.

A HIGHLY RESPECTED SCHOOL HAS TOP-NOTCH PROFESSORS

Many U.S. presidents come from "top-notch" schools and we both know that they're not created equal. Some are good leaders. Some are good followers. And some are just good at raising taxes for the people who can't afford them in the first place.

Further, college administrators are reluctant to provide information about their schools since the media started ranking them. No one wants to get shafted in public for all to see, not surprising. Even still, the ranking of colleges by U.S. News is not verified and critics say that some "reviewers" falsify or sway data.[iv] Some reviewers aren't honest with their answers and, for example, donations from alumni count as a form of customer satisfaction. To cheat the system, some colleges have spread a single donation over several years to bring a college's ranking up.

With that in mind, highly respected schools dwell in a society that's not perfect. Therefore, perfection is unattainable. Still, they have to meet the demand for the several hundred, if not thousands, students who apply to their colleges each year. So they have to relax their professional standards with low-notch professors. Correction. They *must* lower their standards to meet with the demand.

SINCE THE OUTSIDE CAMPUS IS BEAUTIFUL, THE INSIDE OF THE SCHOOL IS BEAUTIFUL

This is simply judging a book by its cover, although admittedly, some title pages beg for a slash through!

An attractive campus can be a sign that the gardener is paid well, but nothing else. Beauty is only skin deep, so ask yourself, 'Would you rather have a lovely campus and lackluster professors, or a tore-up-from-the-floor-up campus and Nobel prize winning professors?'

RACISM DOESN'T EXIST IN COLLEGE

College students live in a world with the rest of us (okay then, most of us). Many come from different lifestyles, cultures and parts of the world. They bring with them their discrimination, prejudices and quirks. They suffer from the ills of general society—including racism—even at top schools. During the writing of this book, a hangman's noose was found on an African-American professor's door at Columbia University in New York City, one of the top tier schools in the country.[v] No school is immune to racism, though most of them try to encourage diversity on campus.

COLLEGE STUDENTS HAVE A HIGHER EDUCATION LEVEL THAN NON-COLLEGE STUDENTS

Granted, the goal of college is not only for students to receive a college degree, but to receive an education. Students will be exposed to things that they hadn't imagined like where the first writings appeared; the philosophic thought of Plato and Socrates; Is global warming really occurring and how humans play a role; and how to implement the Pigeon Hole Principle within a math-related class (don't worry, it's not as intimidating as it sounds).

Non-college students can read the same books and materials that college students read. That is, they can if they *want* too. The trouble is that most people don't go out of their way to seek this kind of knowledge on a regular basis. They don't assign themselves research papers. They don't wake up at nine o'clock in the morning to review Freudian's theory from a psychology textbook then tests themselves on it. People tend to read what interests them and toss the things they dread. It's completely normal. College students can't do that because professors will make sure they don't.

COLLEGE STUDENTS GAIN 15 POUNDS THEIR FIRST YEAR, THE "FRESHMAN 15"

Some students gain 15 pounds their first year of college. Food in the cafeteria is not exactly home cooking. It's fast food. If you're going to cheat on your diet, the food should be divine, not taste like a chamomile tea box, like the food in some school cafeterias.

Yet, students don't have to gain the "Freshman 15." There is no rule that says students can't eat off campus. Some fast-food joints have grilled meats and soup and salad alternatives. But eating healthy doesn't mean not eating. It's a lifestyle choice. And unless you cut out eating at a restaurant altogether, forever, you have to be in a position to choice wisely. If you're confronted with pizza, try to load up with veggie toppings.

COLLEGE IS FOR PLANNERS

Of course, college is for planners. How else would you know what to major in, unless you planned four years ahead? Then again, you could plan two years ahead by taking your core classes first.

IF YOU GO TO CLASS, YOU'LL AUTOMATICALLY PASS

With going to class, surely you'll get some of the best information possible to maximize your learning experience. You can ask your professor to clarify lectures with questions if you don't understand the material. You can also group up with other students to pool your resources. But by no means will you automatically pass a class, simply because you're sitting in your teacher's presence. You definitely get out of college what you put into it. If you've managed to get an "F" out of a class. Most likely, you've put in an "F's" worth of work. But you might get brownie points for your attendance. Some professors take away a percentage of your grade if you are absent a specified number of times.

THE FACULTY IS THERE TO HELP YOU

For the most part, the college faculty is there to help you, though it depends on what your needs are. If you need to know where the student center is, no problem. If you need to know how many more credits you need in order to graduate, you're on your own!

THE LAST YEAR IS THE HARDEST

The last year of college can be the hardest because most students put off having to take chemistry, language studies, math and whatever their weak points are in their final year. Students can minimize this phenomenon by spreading those horror shows over the course of a few semesters. This method can also keep your GPA at an acceptable level, without having it dip from 3.2 to 2.0 or worse.

YOU NEED A 4.0 GPA TO GET A GREAT JOB

Not! Many CEOs wouldn't have become CEOs if that were the case.

PLEDGING A GREEK-LETTERED ORGANIZATION IS THE BEST THING. EVER.

Joining a Greek-letter organization is certainly good for your resume because it shows brother or sisterhood, willingness to work as a team. Not only that, you can make after-college connections, which could help you find a job. But joining any type of organization in college takes up a lot of time, which could throw a pitchfork into your study time and family life. The obligations are massive. You must attend weekly meetings; you must also attend other events that may be outside of your schedule like holding down the door at frat parties. Still interested?

COLLEGE LIFE IS ONE BIG PARTY

If you want a party, head down to the town's fair or the local dive for flamingo lessons because college is not it. College is serious business.

IN THE CLASSROOM

HEATING, COOLING & VENTILATION

Some schools don't have air conditioning. One of the warning signs is the school was built around or before the 1900s. To them, this minor luxury is glorious because true learning can be taught under any circumstances. Mind you, so can heat prostration, otherwise known as a heat stroke!

Heating is not usually a problem, but ventilation can be a tall order in some classrooms. For allergy sufferers, now is the time to get that allergy shot or stock up on over-the-counter medication. Not only does some classrooms not have windows, mopping the floors are usually done once per semester; I'm not kidding.

THE DESKS AND CHAIRS

The desks in the classroom are built for right-handed people, because right-handed people still rule the world. So lefties, like me, you're crap out of luck. You'll have to continue "stretching" your posture like you always have. Nothing new here.

Crayon-colored plastic chairs also dominate the classroom. Remember those? They're still hard and they're still colorful. Things won't be looking on the brighter side of the day when your arthritis kicks in, so be sure to keep Aleeve in your book bag.

STUFF YOU HADN'T THOUGHT OF YET

SCHOOL SUPPLIES

Book bags with wheels attached have got to be the best invention since the girdle panty. Arthritis sufferers will love them—and over 30-year-olds with a bum back.

Item	*Description*
Pens	Erasermate pens are great for writing in-class essays, so you can "erase" your mistakes afterwards.
Pencils	I've always preferred retractable pencils as oppose to have-to-sharpen-with-a-pencil-sharpener pencils.
Notebook with Paper	You'll need a notebook for note taking, but also for in and out of class assignments. Professors prefer

	notebooks with clean edges; that is, if you want a *clean* grade.
Dictionary	Do I need to explain why you need this one?
Calculator	Math classes can be stubborn, so why bother with calculating 5684 divided by 79 in your head?
Post-it® Notes and Flags	These items are good for sticking inside your textbooks.
Small Stapler or Paper Clips	In-class essays can be long
Aspirin	Pain killers for headaches or body aches while your professor is lecturing for three hours.
Band-Aids	For in-school cuts and scrapes. Remember, college kids are contagious!
Anti-bacterial Wipes	It's not uncommon for the school's restroom to run out of soap. Coincidently, when you're in there.
9 x 12 Bookbag, minimum	A sheet of paper is at least eight and a half by eleven inches. Do you see the correlation?
USB Memory Device	A USB memory device is for file saving from a computer and transport because having a "diskette" is way too old school. Some of your classes will

	actually be in the computer lab.

Buy textbooks on the first day of class or email your professors ahead of time. The number of books available at the school bookstore does not equal the number of students registered for a particular class. Some students buy their books from other students or at online stores like Amazon or EBay. In which case, the bookstore doesn't want to end up holding more stock than the demand.

RESALE VALUE OF TEXTBOOKS

Sometimes professors are just mean. And the school bookstore's personnel looks like the childhood monster that gallivanted from your closet as a child. You buy a book, oh, let's say for $130, a brand spankin' new paperback. Then, after the semester is over, the bookstore offers to pay you $40 for the said book. Or worse, after you've purchased a $65 book for a business class and you try to resell it to the bookstore, you get this kind of lip: "We're sorry, but this is the old edition and we can't buy it back."

Unfortunately, this happens a lot and there is not much you can do about it, other than use the textbook in the library or try to find the book online at places like EBay or Amazon. You could always organize a protest with your fellow budding students to demand that the professors use books that are up to date with a higher resale value. But then again, you could always sell the book yourself on EBay.

READING GLASSES

My vision wasn't "poor" until I started reading text the size of a Battledore-Wing, Fairy Fly. With that said, you should start picking out reading glasses if you haven't already. This is not to say that you need glasses (of course not!). This is to say that most textbooks try to squeeze in as much text as possible with eight-point fonts, so they can save on trees—or production costs.

PATIENCE. AND LOTS OF IT

I have a theory, so hear me out. College is the breeding ground for red tape and bureaucracy. The students go on to become government workers, business administrators and teachers even. They learn their professional skills in a classroom, by doing, and by watching others… like the people behind the counters and how these people conduct their business. Because business stinks!

The lines are long. No one knows anything, so they shift the responsibility onto the next (wo)man. So breathe deeply when you encounter this hedonistic behavior. Say to yourself, 'I am here for one thing, and one thing only. That (wo)man (*finger-pointing optional*) behind the counter will not rile me up as to scream!'

POINTS TO REMEMBER

- Send for high school and college transcripts of other colleges that you attended at least three months in advance.

- Save your utility bills from the past year to prove residency. Otherwise, pay up to 100 percent more for tuition.

- Round up your immunizations records for MMR (measles, mumps & Rubella) proof. This could take up to six months to get if it's been a long time and your records are down in the basement.

- Get an allergy shot if you are allergic to dust.

- On your first day of school, check out neighborhood and campus' restaurants, so you can plan your meals. That is, if you don't want to gain weight.

- School supplies come in handy: Erasermate Pens, pencils, notebook, dictionary, calculator, Post-it® Notes, paper clips, aspirin, Band-Aids, anti-bacterial wipes, 9x12 or larger book bag and a USB memory hard-drive.

3 SCHEDULING, YES, YOU ACTUALLY HAVE TO SHOW UP

Full-time or part-time? That is the question. Twelve credit hours or more is considered full-time (four to six classes). Making it to class everyday is the easy bit because the real work begins when you walk through the door of your home—all day, and all night; it's called homework. You still want to go?

Eighty-four percent of Americans say that higher education is extremely important. Sixty-six percent of non-college graduates wish they had gone.[vi]

If you have small children, you're going to have to make childcare accommodations. Some colleges have on-site daycare facilities for students with small children free of charge or for a small nominal fee. You have to get locked into this privilege early on. It'll fill up quickly. This should be amongst the first order of business.

Can't fit going to college into your schedule with a family? Consider night or weekend classes. You can take a few classes after work or in your spare time. Most colleges offer this option. But be forewarned, the likelihood of you rolling out of bed on a Saturday or Sunday morning is not highly probable. Night classes can be a drag if you're in bed by nine o'clock or have children who aren't old enough to entertain themselves.

If you just can't manage to afford anything else trumping up in your already hectic schedule, consider online classes, otherwise known as distance learning. Parlaying on the sofa with your laptop, eating chocolate truffles while chugging down a beer, is the right way to listen to a professor's lecture. So if you get bored, you can just tell him or her that your computer crashed (disclaimer: I am not responsible for the outcome if you pull this fast one). In most cases, you will get your assignments via the college's Web site or sent via email. You can even take your exams from your home. However, some colleges may require you to come into the institution for exams or have them proctored from another institution. Sure, online classes are convenient, but don't think for a second that your homework load will be just as forgiving. In fact, several students who have taken online classes have told me that these courses are much harder than the tradition courses.

You also have the option of going to summer school, so you can graduate faster, not that you don't enjoy your peers. Time is something that's valuable to you. You'd like to be out of there before you start collecting from your retirement fund. Don't you?

If things start falling apart in your life, missing a few days per semester is normal. And for the most part, built into the system. Some colleges allow up to eight class hours of absence, approximately six to eight days per semester. Some colleges don't mind if students don't show up at all, as long as exams and assignments have passing grades. But lectures are important. Oftentimes, you won't have to study as hard as you would have if you didn't attend regularly. In all likelihood, the professor will review the same materials that are in the book. You'll read it once and hear it again.

Once you've chosen a schedule, get a campus map because it will take some time to familiarize yourself with the college grounds. You're guaranteed to lose 15 minutes each day, circling around to the spot you left five minutes prior. Not only that, if you've got a bum knee or back, you'll need to cut yourself some slack.

POINTS TO REMEMBER

- Full-time or part-time? Colleges have finally accepted that there is no such thing as a one-size-fits-all curriculum for college students. We come from all lifestyles with different demands on our lives. Your schooling options include:

4 HOW IN THE WORLD ARE YOU GOING TO PAY FOR THIS?

Tuition is going to cost you, even if your school selection is a state- or city-owned college. Teachers are still underpaid and inflation hibernates for no one. Books will cost from $200 to $400 per semester, so make sure you tack on this "hidden" fee.

Travel expenses, lunch and do-dads can add on a chunk too. Occasionally, your professors might ask you to buy something that you'll never use again like graphing paper or a jackhammer, although the jackhammer might come in handy for the re-finishing project that you've never got around to.

WAYS TO CUT COST

To cut cost, analyze your life for things you don't *need* like cable or satellite TV (is there anything on, anyway?), cell phones, Neflix and weekly Chinese take-out—pizza too. These things can add hundreds of dollars per month to your expenses. Some things like Starbucks, you do in fact need. So make room for this one.

Another way to cut cost is to sell your vehicle and take public transportation––unless you live in a small town and the nearest college is 60 miles away; but do you think you can hitch a ride? You'll save on car payments, insurance and gas. That's a hefty hunk of change per month. And enough for college tuition. Ask yourself, 'Which is more important: that Volkswagen out back or a piece of paper?' You do the math.

If you're not willing to part with your vehicle, consider moving into a cheaper apartment if you lease. You could always re-mortgage the house and live on Ramen Noodles if you own a home. College is an investment. Oftentimes, rent or mortgage is the most expensive monthly payment of any household. But think of it as a stock option: It's low-risk and has a high return in the shortest amount of time. What broker can offer you that? The admission's office can!

TOAST! YOUR EDUCATION IS ON THE HOUSE

Grant money, a.k.a. free money, is worth a shot. It's better than gold because you don't have to pay it back. What's there not to like?

The Federal Pell Grant is based on financial need. The amount dispersed to each student is dependent on expectant family income, tuition cost, and whether you are a full- or part-time student. To determine your eligibility, you must fill out a Free Application for Federal Student Aid (FAFSA), which is due May 1 of any given year. The catch, you must not have already received a bachelor's degree or plan to attend school for more than five years, in the case of some majors. Then again, if you've already gotten a degree, you wouldn't need this book, now would you?

Gather up your income tax returns, bank statements, investment papers, retirement plan information and the kitchen sink. Also, to be eligible, you need to have a high-school diploma or GED; get satisfactory grades (no F's please); no previous student loan defaults; and is a U.S. citizen.

Scholarships are also available for almost all majors and hobbies, from chemistry majors to hand-knitting hobbyists. Scholarship information can be found on your chosen school's Web site, that'll direct you to another Web site, in which their probably getting kickbacks for (on a side note: you haven't heard this from me). It's probably legit if the school recommends it. But I have to tell you, looking for scholarships will be like putting your head into a vice unless you're seriously down on your luck, or you can wing an essay like the Harry Potter author, JK Rowling.

SCHOLARSHIP SCAMS

Let's face it. As long as you live in a free nation, confidence persons will exercise their free will to scam unsuspecting students. According to the Federal Trade Commission, students should look out for these buzz words when looking for scholarships:

- *"The scholarship is guaranteed or your money back."*

- *"You're a finalist,"* in a contest you've never entered.

- *"I just need your credit card or bank account number to hold this scholarship."* Right.

Most people know by now not to give credit card or banking information over the phone to a person, particularly a stranger, who doesn't need it. Still, thousands of people get taken for a ride to what they believe is a chocolate factory offering free goodies. You shouldn't have to pay money to get free money.

The median earnings of a high school graduate or GED recipient are $25,360. The median earning of a college grad with a bachelor's degree is $42,404.

EMPLOYEE SPONSORED DOUGH

Still haven't found any money? Your employer may come to the rescue with a tuition assistance program. Why wouldn't they? They want smart employees. They can award you up to $5,250, tax-free, though some employers will require that you maintain a minimum GPA (Grade Point Average) or the degree of your choice must be work-related. For example, suppose you're a retail store clerk, majoring in art history will not get you a raise at the end of the year. But if you're a retail salesperson, majoring in retail management will surely make your current manager spike your coffee with alcoholic offerings to tarnish your credibility. Check with your employer's human resources department for their policy.

MILITARY VETERANS

If you're a veteran of the United States armed forces, you may qualify for the Montgomery GI Bill. Spouses may also be eligible for benefits via the DEA (Dependent Educational Assistance). VA benefits are not currently taxable income, but I'm sure the IRS is working on a way to garnish this subsidy.

Long Pham, who writes a personal finance blog, http://www.budgetforwealth.com, is a military vet, serving in the Army National Guard and the Iraq War, suggests that vets starting at age 25 submit a FAFSA application every year, even if they are receiving education benefits such as the GI Bill. Typically, a vet has to be 24 years of age or older to be considered independent. Until then, they have to include their parent's income on the FAFSA, which can disqualify them for grants or subsidized loans. However, veterans are considered independent, no matter the age. This opportunity makes it easier for the veteran to qualify for grants and/or subsidized loans because they don't have to include their parents income on the FAFSA application. Ta-da!

Veterans may also receive credit for courses acquired within the military. And then there's always the option to test out of various courses via CLEP exams. Some colleges are more receptive to accepting military credits than others. A CUNY school, Brooklyn College, assured me that they were very generous about accepting military credits. See your chosen college's, veterans affairs' office and bring your military paperwork, stating as to your discharge. You can find more about the GI Bill at their Web site at http://www.gibill.va.gov/.

Kathryn "Katie" E. Schellenberg, Esq., CEO of BeyondTutoring.com, has worked with many vets and nontraditional students and has some tips to share:

"Chiefly, I think that student veterans have trouble readjusting to student life to a greater degree than a traditional student. I think they feel less connected to student population being away from the service at least at first, and going from a very regimented environment to one that is far less so can be jarring," she said.

"I think community colleges I have seen are a great option for student veterans for several reasons: Interestingly, I have seen more veterans services on community colleges than on university campuses; Because there is a wide range of students in a wide swath of ages, veterans can thrive in classes; It is also somewhat less intense, more practical, and can have more practical class offerings. Although some veterans are looking for the four year college experience, a community college offers certificate programs, AA programs and other career programs that would help a veteran acclimatize into society."

SENIORS
Some colleges offer discounts to seniors. This discount can range up to 30 percent, with other special services for seniors only.

A PENNY SAVED IS A PENNY EARNED

The Coverdell Education Savings Account is one option for students with special needs. The funds in this trust are not tax deductible, but the interest grows tax-free. The maximum income is approximately $110,000 to $220,000 for joint returns. Contributions can be made, up to $2,000, if the beneficiary is under 18 years old. Funds must also be drawn by the time the "student" is 30 years old. So that doesn't apply to some of you! But… if you are a "special needs beneficiary" then you may qualify no matter your age. After smoldering on hold with the IRS for 37 minutes, they still couldn't give me a definition of special needs; it hadn't been published yet. You can find more information within the IRS's 970 yellow-page-of-a-pamphlet publication at www.irs.gov.

Pinching from your Roth or traditional IRA account is your last resort. Indeed, you'll have an education, but you could be chowing on Iams Active Maturity™ in your golden years if you're not careful. Using your IRA account to fund you or your family's education is allowed without a 10 percent tax penalty. However, you may have to pay an income tax on the withdrawn funds for this privilege. You knew there had to be a catch.

There's always the late-night stop at the black jack table at the casino. Hey, don't knock it until you've tried it. Just don't lay the house deed on the line.

SIGNING YOUR LIFE AWAY WITH LOANS

Fortunately, most colleges have a payment-plan system like AMS[1] (Academic Management Services), which is owned by the Sallie Mae Corporation. I mean, come on, who just happens to have a couple thousand dollars stuffed underneath their mattress. Oh, you do? Well then, I'm referring to the people who can barely squeeze their newfound wisdom into their budget. AMS is not based on financial need, so don't worry if your household makes more than a gazillion dollars per year. You pay approximately a $35 setup fee and the company breaks your payments over the semester term. They even accept people with strained credit histories. Sweet huh? I've exercised this little

[1] TEXT BOX: www.tuitionpay.com

thingamajig throughout my college tenure. And without it, let's just say I'd still be scrubbing dishes and hauling laundry full-time.

The downside of AMS is that they break the payments over the course of the semester. Period. Most semesters run from three to four months long. So, say, you have a $2,500 tuition payment and you have four months to pay it. With my dismal calculations—math was never one of my strongpoints—you have $625 monthly payments. "Holy cow!" you say. "That's about as much as my mortgage!" That it certainly is, which means you'd have to cut back on weekly facials or Saturday afternoons at the racing track. Imagine paying this house-and-the-kitchen-sink-along-with-the-floorboards payment for the next few years. Fortunately, it beats the alternative, which is not going at all. You also have to sign up every semester if you want assistance. Or you can sign up for one semester and not the next. There is no long-term contract, so you can bounce in and out.

Four-year college students acquired an average of $15,000 to $20,000 in debt by the time they graduated.[vii]

You could always take out a low-interest student loan if you still don't have the dough. Guaranteed student loans (GSL) are subsidized by the federal government. The interest rates on these loans are usually lower than private-based loans. They are, in fact, "guaranteed." Albeit this is still a loan and must be paid back, but with a little more wiggle room. You can request a "forbearance," which is simply delaying the date that you are to begin your first payment if you are in a financial squeeze. And if you ignore payment requests, the loan can become delinquent, which will go on your credit reports for the next seven years.

A bankruptcy cannot exempt a student loan. The government can also sanction your tax refund to pay the balance if owed (there goes that new dishwasher!). If you've defaulted on a GSL in the past, you won't be eligible this time around unless you've settled that other nightmare.

THE UPSIDE

At least all or part of a college education is tax deductible: tuition, books and college-related expenses. I knew that'd get your heartbeat purring. It sure got my husband's wallet slaphappy. But check with the IRS for up to date information. Oh, come on, they're friendly over the phone.

POINTS TO REMEMBER

- Don't forget to factor in the cost of textbooks. They can add up to $400 to your tuition bill each semester.

- To sign up for a Federal Pell Grant (free money!), fill out the Free Application for Federal Student Aid (FAFSA) by May 1 of any given year. Some colleges are relaxed about this deadline and they might cut you some slack after the due date. The only thing they can do is say no.

- Scholarships can be found on your school's Web site. DO NOT EVER PAY MONEY FOR SCHOLARSHIP INFORMATION. EVER.

- Check with your current employer about tuition assistance. Most likely, the courses would have to be job related.

- Try not to tap into your IRA account to pay for college. Only if you have to.

- Black jack, anyone?

- Loans aren't all bad, but it's still a loan. So treat it like one.

5 WHAT WILL YOU WEAR?

No man is an island, old wise one; you can't get through college alone. The beauty of youth—other than the fact it's wasted on the young—is that most young students accept just about everyone, as long as you don't resemble their parents.

With that said, it's time to update your wardrobe. And since you're older, most likely you won't have a similar cash-flow problem like other students. You can out shop any acne-prone pubescent. Though keep in mind, this will be a new expense, one that neither you nor your spouse had anticipated. You will need at least $200 to get decent college garb. I've managed to put together a hit list, making your transition smoother.

HOW NOT TO BE COOL

- Wearing 70s or 80s fashions is a sure fire way to send young, budding students fleeing in the opposite direction, even though updated versions are coming back, just not original materials. Your old clothes can get a second life on EBay and should! Suppose you can't afford a new wardrobe, take $200 and shop on EBay. You can always spread this fee out and buy one to two outfits at a time.

- Stay away from low-rise jeans—unless you want everyone sitting behind you to check out your butt cleavage. Guys, this should be understood. But I'll say it anyway, no hip-huggers for men either. Did you get a vivid image in your mind's eye just like I did? Never mind.

- "Easy-Fit" jeans will make you look like a mom or a pop, not a student—not to mention it'll make you look like you're smuggling books in there. Comfort is key, but sacrificing fashion for it is a crime against humanity! It you must wear "easy" anything, then go for straight- or boot-leg denims, or the Gap's "Curvy fit" for the ladies. These cut styles will certainly hide saddlebags with the straight cuts. Oh, and guys, please place your pants at your natural waist, not your chest, thank you.

- Hushpuppies and Easy Spirit shoes are for the office, not a college environment (don't give me that look). These shoes scream: Look at me people! I'm a mature adult going back to college. Not only that, I've managed to make a dork of myself! Is that the message you'd like to honk? Shoes that are far more comfortable exist that don't attach themselves to house pets. Loafers, not the penny kind, are okay or you can never go wrong with sneakers. For the ladies, up-to-date flats with arch support insoles are always safe because backpacks and stilettos don't mix. You're going to be one hauling jackass.

- Are you a hippie? You might just fit right in! The hippie style is relaxed without trying too hard. Many college students are right at home in jeans and t-shirts, although tie-dye shirts might be somewhat of a rarity.

THE BARE NECESSITIES

- Blue eyeshadow is a definite no-no because your eyelids are not where they used to be. *Ahem*, mature women should stick to earthy tones. The rule of thumb is the less make-up you wear, the younger you'll look.

- Wear your nails short and natural if you can bear it. There won't be much time for primping. Plus, week-old nail polish wouldn't exactly make you the pillar of the college community, although it might raise your caste level with the kids who wear black lipstick.

- For men, a mustache is okay, but it can make you look up to 10 years older. So, say, you want to nab a 20-something-year-old hottie. If you're single, it's time to donate that wooly mammoth to science. Then again, some young women have been known to fancy older men on other planets in the solar system!

- Mohawks and mullets are optional, but big Texas hair and Jerri Curls are not. Do you see where this is going?

Points to Remember

- Low-rise jeans are not practical for college.

- Easy-fit jeans are not practical for anyone.

- House-pet names shoes belong in an office.

6 MAJOR PAINS: CHOOSING YOUR CLASSES

SHUFFLING YOUR OPTIONS

Read the descriptions of your classes before you sign up. Some of them may not be what you think or the title of the class may be a gross representation of its contents. *Intro to Poetry*, for example, may cover the history of poets from the 18th Century, not about learning to write poetry for the 21st Century. And when you decide upon a college major, read those descriptions too. Look at the list of courses that are actually required for your major.

Once you've actually gotten around to picking a major, make sure you're taking the right path in getting that promotion you'd always wanted, or for a new career prospect. You'd hate to smolder in college for longer than you have to. And for the love of god, don't major in pottery or sculpting. College is way too expensive to dove into your hobbies. Major in something so you can have a real job to pay the mortgage. You know, to the people at the bank who actually own your home?

If you're still undecided on a major,[2] take all the core classes first. Core classes are building-block courses that are required for all majors. Most colleges feel that these "starter courses" help students become well-rounded graduates (I have my own theories, thank you). For example: You can hover around the water cooler at work while talking about how music has transformed from the monophonic, plain songs like Gregorian chants to the polyphonic sounds of Patti Smith. Mentioning Britney Spears instead can really make you sound up to speed.

The cores will usually take two to three semesters to complete (for you slow buggers, that's about one-and-a-half years). Most of them will seem like a waste of time—that's because most of them are—but this is what it'll take to drool over that glossy diploma you've always wanted.

CAN YOU GUESS THESE CELEBRITIES' MAJORS?

    A. Richard Nixon

    B. Denzel Washington

    C. Martha Stewart

    D. Garth Brooks

    E. Michael Jordan

    F. Oprah Winfrey

A.) History. B.) Journalism. C.) History & Architectural History. D.) Advertising. E.) Geology. F.) Speech & Drama

* *Source: "How to Choose a College Major" Linda Landis Andrews – McGraw-Hill 2006 and MSN Encarta.*

Talk to an academic counselor at the school if you're still confused about all this. They can probe your brain with questions about your likes, dislikes and where you see yourself in five to ten years. I guess you can just ask yourself that right now. Where do you see yourself in 10 years? Are you good with children? Do you like dealing with people? Do you thrive under pressure and lay flaccid when the pressure's off? Are you a chatterbox or a lonesome dove? Imagine yourself doing that job, being that job when deciding on a major. Supposing you are a chatterbox, then festering in a back office as an accountant would probably not suit you. And don't think of becoming an attorney if stage fright smothers your wherewithal.

Go prepared with a hit list before you visit their office. Things will go smoothly—and they'll have you signing up to be an astrophysicist in no time. With that said, bolt up from the chair if an academic counselor tells you that you cannot do or be something. If your heart is in it and you have the dedication, why can't you?

Whether you've decided already or not, you will have to declare something by your second year. For those of you who already have college classes under your belt, you must declare straight away. At first, most students take the easy way out and declare "liberal arts" as a major. Translation: "I haven't the slightest idea what I want to do with my life, but I do know my parents sent me to college for something." Don't worry. Most students get an idea of what they want to do and what they don't want to do within two semesters. The class ranges will vary. The core classes, which everyone has to take, will test your enthusiasm on which subjects you like best. I chose journalism because it kept me writing. I love to write, perform research and communicate with people. I did not choose creative writing because I knew I needed a steady job; I could always write books on the side.

ADULT CONTINUING EDUCATION

Adult continuing education courses are fun. In fact, I've taken a few myself. The duration of classes are short and the course instructors apply a practical, hands-on approach with less theory. What's not to like? Well... I can think of one thing. You won't receive college credit for these courses. And if you do, the class credit may equal to "one." You still want to take that typing course?

PRE-USED MAJORS

Returning students who want to pursue their previous majors need to make sure the major's requirements haven't changed. Some majors will require more classes or different classes to fulfill your graduation requirements. Believe it or not, college institution's class rosters aren't written in asphalt because education is fluid. Out with the old and in with the new is the *new* thing for many colleges and universities. For example, if your previous college major was psychiatry, and studying the psychoanalytic theory of Freud, you might not be able to find it in the psychology department anymore. According to an American Psychoanalytic Association study, many psychology departments across the country, and textbooks alike, treat Freud's theory as a "historical artifact instead of an ongoing movement and a living, evolving process."[viii]

Many law schools have also changed their curriculums, with new courses and clinical programs. Columbia, Harvard, Stanford and the University of New Mexico law schools have taken the lead. Previously, many law schools have concentrated on case studies, things that have already been done. These schools cited that they'd like to keep up to date with the times, as there are many laws that have not yet been presented to a judge like several kinds of torts and contracts. Also, many lawyers were trained with generalized knowledge, but these schools would like to encourage students to take courses outside of their majors, so they can specialize in a particular field.[ix] So if you've been trying to convince your spouse for the past few years to return to college, it's time to step up your sales pitch.

SWITCHING MAJORS

Switching majors is a feat reserved for the criminally insane. Okay, you've got me, but I've only done it three times during my life-long quest to finish college. My first major was accounting, then psychology, journalism, then I ended up with a degree in communications. A mixed bag, huh? My transcript looks like a tossed salad mixed with fruit, peanuts and split peas.

Get a plan and stick to it. You could be left with several do-nothing credits. Think about your major long and hard before choosing one. Think about you sitting in the office of your choice. Then ask yourself, 'Can I live with this measly salary they're paying me?'

= Personal Anecdote =

Most likely, an employer will not see your transcript. However, they just might. After transferring schools four times (two were junior colleges; the other two were senior colleges), an internship I had applied for wanted to see my transcripts. I was mortified! Surely, they'd think I was unstable. Not only that, my school tenure, as stated on my transcripts, started in 1993, long before most 20-year-olds were in high school.

I needed a plan. I needed to get out of this mess. On its own, my transcript(s) wouldn't have past the scrutiny of a judgmental employer. So I had to explain the lapses in time, the several colleges. I did that in my cover letter:

As a non-traditional student, I went back to college at 32 years old, originally dropping out at 19 when the combination of full-time school and work provided a burden. I chose to work to keep my first apartment, not wanting to return to my parent's home after I had acquired the taste of independence. Later on, I realized that an education was important. Not only is knowledge power, but also college provided one with a career, not just a job.

Since going back over two years ago—starting at a junior college—I knew I loved to write, so I decided on journalism because it kept me writing. It didn't take long for me to join the student newspaper. Later, I wrote several articles for the local newspaper for a year, while still in school.

While majoring in journalism at Brooklyn College, a senior college, I knew I wanted to pursue public relations as a career goal. I wrote for the student newspaper to keep my writing skills sharp, and then started an internship as PR support to gain more valuable knowledge. My colleagues suggested I get a communications degree as opposed to a journalism degree. It was still not too late, but I had to make a decision right away. The next semester, the only courses left—outside of my core credits—were my "major" classes. But Brooklyn College didn't offer a communications degree. I had already taken the sole "Intro to PR" class they offered. Where would I go? After consulting with my advisors, The City College was the answer.

As of Spring 2008, I'm continuing my education in communications, namely advertising & public relations, at The City College. I'm looking forward to my anticipated graduation date of May 2009. I'm also looking forward to gaining as much knowledge as I can about my chosen career.

Thank you for considering me as an intern.

THE MINORS

Pick a minor in something completely different to your major, but somewhat related. Doing so will make you more marketable. For example, suppose your major is accounting, minor in sociology. A business major? Minor in nutrition. If your major is journalism, minor in marketing. The goal is to maximize your job-market opportunities. During my junior year in college, journalists were downsized right and left. It didn't faze me. I had other skills that were highly marketable, like marketing. I was not only a writer, but I had business skills. I could be an editor, a public relations professional, a market research analyst, or create market-planning documents. From my journalism training, I was also a research specialist. I could find jobs in up to six different professions. And if I really put more thought into it, I could wiggle my credentials into the culinary arts.

SKILLS

Not only will you need at least a bachelor's degree to get ahead in this world, but also you'll need skills, technical know-how. What good is a career in veterinary technology if you don't know how to use a computer? Better yet, specific software programs that are standard in the business.

A good way to figure out what you need is to browse the online job circuit in your field. In my field, I had seen several programs repeated like Filemaker Pro, Bacons, Microsoft Word, PowerPoint, Excel, Adobe InDesign, and a slew of others. If my school didn't offer the workshop, I downloaded a trial version and taught myself with a how-to book from the library. The more skills you have, the more palatable your resume looks to an employer.

SHUFFLING AROUND YOUR OPTIONS

Registration happens in hierarchies: The seniors register first, then the juniors, then sophomores, and so on. As a new student, your registration date will be appointed after everyone else has picked over the classes. This is your gift from college—but you can thank them later.

If you can, take classes you enjoy first. These classes can leave you with the right impression about whether or not you're cut out for this college business in the first place. In the second place, you won't waste too much hard cash and you can stow away your college aspirations if you're not ready. Also, taking these courses first will get you back into the swing of things. Suppose math or physics is your mania, then dive right in, although I wouldn't recommend this buoyant feat. You could be out of there faster than they can process your tuition payment.

Some classes require "prerequisites," which are building blocks, the basics. The high-ranking professors don't want to spend their precious time going over every little detail—the dumbed down version—of a particular subject. The lower-on-the-totem-pole professors usually teach these courses. You'll learn a broad-even stroke of the subject then specialize with upper classes.

Taking several random classes could well veer your graduation plans into a ditch. You only have approximately 120 credits to play with for a four-year degree and much less than that for electives. So use them prudently. The last thing you'd want to have is 20 left-over-do-nothing credits. They certainly won't transfer into graduate school. Oh, thinking of going to grad school? Let's take this thing one at a time Steadfast Stacy.

Balance the course load with theory and practical classes. Your brain can only handle so much information at once. Imagine this, you're taking algebra, geometry and chemistry at the same time... That's not what you want to do! I usually rate classes with one to four stars: One is the easiest; two is relatively easy, but I'd have to write at least one BIG term paper during the course; three stars means the course is hefty, somewhere in the middle; and a four-star course means I have to reserve that one class its own semester. To illustrate, I had planned to take geology and advertising & direct marketing together because I knew geology would require lots of reading and mind twisting I-don't-knows. Marketing wouldn't do that to me. If you're taking English classes and writing is not your forte, take something like "drawing" with it and two- or three-star courses to level your sanity.

Try not to pick courses that are too early or too late and you know you can't show up. You're making a commitment here, so be responsible and do the right thing. Give a grace period for the baby sitter to have car trouble, even though you know that he or she is hung-over because they stayed out all night. And just say no if you're not an eight-o'clock-in-the-morning person. Look for another class, although sometimes you might have to bend this rule. There may be *one* class in *one* section that you must take in order to graduate. I shall call this, "having an out-of-body experience." Your body is festering in the classroom while your mind is sprawled out in your king-size bed.

Scheduling classes right after the other can put you into the "I'm-going-to-school mode." This is a good thing. You'll need at least two to three months until it sinks in that you're actually the one in Romper-Room Middle School. Try to schedule as many of them on the same day as possible, so you can take mini-vacations during the week. Well, from school anyway, but that'll also mean you have to catch up on household chores. Then, next semester try to have at least a one-hour gap in between classes so you can check out the school cafeteria and see what your peers are up to. Student watching is far more advantageous than, say, watching Law & Order. You can also use this time to study or perform research in the library, like catching up on that paper that you hadn't started writing yet.

CAUTION

Don't get too excited about those fancy classes with the fancy titles that you'd like to sign up for. Not every course is offered every semester. In fact, reading the school's catalog is about as accurate as my mother's psychic abilities. The semester schedule is the best way to go on this one. You can have it mailed to you, free of charge, before you sign up for classes at your chosen college. The downside is that if you don't choose that particular school, you've just put yourself on their junk-mail list.

www.ratemyprofessor.com is a place where you can view your professor's report card, which is wickedly rated by the students.

OTHER CLASSES YOU MIGHT HAVE TO TAKE

For Baby Boomers, take at least one computer, how-to course. Otherwise, your preparedness would be like a carpenter showing up to re-do the floorboards without a hammer. Then again, you could always lend him or her that jackhammer your professor made you buy.

Everything has gone hi-tech: registering online, getting school-related announcements sent via email, and even your grades. I know you've been putting it off. You just haven't gotten around to it yet. Right? Learning computers was a scary thing for me, at first. I stared at a "mouse" for 30 minutes before I could figure out what its use was. It's hard to keep up, especially with ongoing innovations.

LANGUAGE

¿Habla Español? Some colleges require proficiency in a language other than English in order for you to graduate. High-school foreign language counts, so you're probably off the hook in that case. If you've watched Russian Bay Watch on occasion, then you'll simply have to demonstrate your multi-language abilities, via an exam.

Spanish is not the only language available, even though it's probably the most useful in the United States. Polish, Chinese, German and other languages are an option, especially if you've been dying to tell your neighbors off in French.

LIFE CREDIT: OLDER AND WISER?

As you get older, you realize that even though you weren't in a classroom setting, you've acquired knowledge nonetheless. You've acted as a sponge, taking in news' broadcasts, magazine articles (yep, even if they were about gardening or how-to-put-together-my-son's-Schwinn-bicycle). All this "life knowledge" will come in handy. A lot of the course material will be drawn from it. When I first discovered I knew stuff, I was on cloud 47; that is, until I had to take algebra. Can we move on now?

Use your worldly knowledge to give you an edge. You can get a "life credit" at some colleges, albeit you may have to take an exam to acquire it. The College-Level Examination Program (CLEP) is one option. You can "test out" of courses by taking this exam via a testing site and earn up to 12 college credits per exam, choosing from several subject areas. I did a quick search on www.collegeboard.com to see if my college offered the CLEP. They did. So yours might be there too.

At the same time, if you know that you could brush up on your scholastic skills, don't test out of classes. Start at the bottom, so you can maximize your learning potential. And no, you probably won't get a life-credit claiming that you're simply older and wiser (I tried this one to no avail), and for house management, although I'd look into this because it might fall under the home-economics program. Technical training counts; this doesn't mean learning how to program the DVR either.

Points to Remember

- Can you get a real job with your degree choice?
- Are you undecided on a major? Take core classes first to buy some time.

- Some adult continuing education courses don't offer college credit.

- Switching majors is your last resort.

- Pick a minor in something related, but different than your major.

- Skills are important too.

- Balance the course load with theory and practical classes.

- Include language courses if required. Take at least one computer course anyway.

- Test out of courses with the College-Level Examination Program (CLEP).

- Check out www.ratemyprofessor.com to check out what your soon-to-be professors have been doing.

7 WHAT HAPPENS NOW?

... IN THE CLASSROOM

As an older student, you get to see what the Department of Education has done to the system. The No Child Left Behind Act of 2001 was implemented to ensure that all students learn at the same pace and no one gets left behind. This Act applies to first and secondary schools, but its promising ability has echoed throughout post-secondary schools as well.

This is good, you say. It depends. If you require a little more explaining to get up to speed—which is highly probable since you're an older student—you don't mind paying higher taxes for the educational system. In fact, you might even send a letter to your local government thanking them for finally getting their acts together. On the other hand, if you're a quick learner, you're in for a treat. Your days will slosh ahead like the little engine that never did. You're compelled to hear the same instruction repeatedly and over again, sparking visions of your professor getting his or her foot stuck between the metro train cars on their way to class.

Fifteen to 35 students could assemble in each class, no personalized attention-grabbers here. The professors simply don't have time to cater to individual needs, so they'll address questions from the census. If you need more help, see the professor after class. They often have office hours for this sort of thing.

ARE YOU IN THE GETTING GOOD GRADES BUSINESS?

College is work. Don't think you can soar your way through this or you'll plummet faster than Seinfeld's ratings after that Michael "Kramer" Richards' fiasco. For me, going back to college was one of the toughest things I had ever done. The unnecessary plodding and poking through one's brain had taken learning to a new level. Surely, the process was unnatural. My brain had been washed, re-washed, and then rung out to dry all wrinkly. I could only recall half of the material that I had learned after the semester was over.

Still, you'll want to maintain an even-heeled GPA (Grade Point Average), a numerical number, which is a combination of the grades you receive from each class. You'd want to shoot for the 3.0 to 4.0 range, which will snugly put you up there with the "A" students. To stay in college—and to keep your grants and scholarships—a 2.0 is minimum, which is a "C" average. Remember "A, B, C's" not "D, F's." But if home-duties are requiring too much of your time, getting a "C" is better than failing altogether, although in most schools, a "D" is actually passing.

Which can also happen, you think you deserve an "A" and your professor keeps trumping a ""B+" your way. Professors do this to keep you motivated. Getting straight "A's" will only make you feel that you're not challenged enough. I say the less work you have to put into it, the better.

So repeat after me when the tough gets going: "This too shall pass. I am empowered. I am strong and confident—even if I'm about to fail this tribulation." Scratch that last part! Some classes might seem easy at first and require very little time until you get that one class that will change your view of college forever. I mean that in a bad way.

College is also about endurance, the will to survive and surface in one piece. College is about learning too. But think about it, the average student spends 33 to 36 credit hours towards their major out of 120 credits total. That's about

11 to 15 classes out of approximately 40 total classes in everything else. Granted, most schools want to create "renaissance" persons, someone who knows a little bit about everything. But no one person excels at everything. The amount of information absorbed in such a short amount of time—with four truckloads of homework, to boot—is about staying power, not intellect.

SOCIALIZATION

Despite being over 30 years old, you can still get caught up in the college life. How? Oh, say, frat parties and joining student clubs and forgetting that you're actually there to learn. Use your head when socializing. Student clubs can be hands-on, so your studies may suffer. You've still got house chores. You may have to run home every night by five o'clock to pick up Jimmy from the babysitter or throw a pot roast into the microwave.

Visiting the school cafeteria, or other public place in the school, might create a sense of belonging without joining student clubs. Even for us older folks, feeling isolated for the next couple of years helps no one, although I sat in the cafeteria a few times and students walked right by me like a solicitor handing out flyers for a toaster-oven give-a-way.

Nalana, 34, Chicago

"I'm very social, but haven't found too many people to socialize with on a regular basis. Mostly, it seems like everyone [in college] is trying to get in and get out; they have other outside things they must take care of that doesn't allow too much socialization outside of or in between classes."

GOOD KARMA WITH THE PROFESSOR

So say you've found a great professor that you'd have sworn was hired just for you: You love their teaching style; you've aced all of their exams; and he or she can't get enough of reading your essays. Somebody loves you up there! You've already decided to take every class this professor offers at the college. You want smooth sailing, and with them, there are no bumpy roads ahead. This is good, right? Wrong.

It's great to have good karma with your professor. In fact, moments like these make all the troll teachers crawl back into the hole in which they came. As you might have already figured out, each professor has different teaching styles. But their knowledge is limited to their experiences and training. In other words, they only know so much and they're teaching you *only* what they know. Branch out and experience what other professors have to offer. You might learn something new along the way.

SELF-REFLECTION

The bright side of all this pandemonium is that independence will be re-found. You've been cuddled in a dark hole for way too long. You'll have a new sense of pride because you're getting things done. You're doing what you've always wanted to do, going back to college. If you have to confront the where-in-the-hell-is-my-spouse phenomenon these days, you can take it. Remind your loved ones how important your education is to the entire family (Warning: Please wipe the smirk from your face when you say this because they will have to pick up some of the slack.)

To try and ease the pressure that may be upon you, include your family members in your academic decision-making processes. For example: "Dear, which class do you think I should take next semester? Biology or philosophy?"

This is a loaded question, of course, because they should avoid choosing philosophy like a bad exit route on Route 66. You'd soon come home examining everything in your lives together: Imagine you and your family sitting in the living room, and all of a sudden, "Honey, why do you think we chose burnt orange for the walls in here as oppose to eggplant?" Your spouse will then peel his or her neck sideways and look at you like bean plants just sprouted from both ears… This one is a little safer: Put your passing exams on the refrigerator (I know, reminds you of when you were in kindergarten, but you are in fact "starting over."). This will let them know that the money you are spending on college is actually getting some use!

POINTS TO REMEMBER

- College is work and you are responsible for your own learning.

- Resilience is one of the qualities to have if you want to attend college.

- Stay focused. You are in college for one reason, to get an education.

- Diversify with professors because one professor is limited to his or her knowledge.

- Get your family involved in college-making decisions. This will help them feel like a part of your new world, which could alleviate stress.

8 THE COURSEWORK SITUATION

REWIRING YOUR MEMORY

Anyone can learn. Granted, it may take your mature brain a little longer than others, but it still holds the capacity to do so. You need to be willing to accept change, throw out all of the old wife's tales and unlearn many things you have learned up until this point. Learning is a life-long, innate phenomenon. All cultures do it[x].

One of the best things about college is that the setting and curriculum are designed to maximize the learning process; well, in most colleges anyway. Oftentimes, the head of a department gives professors a list of objectives for students to learn within a specific time frame. Drawing from previous experiences and questioning your own assumptions and mores—particularly if your assumptions are drawn from backyard knowledge—can propel the learning concept. For instance, if you still think that nine planets exist, knowledge says otherwise because there are now eight; Pluto has been exiled.

The art of learning further entails an acceptance that some things are not within reach[xi]. You will not learn everything in the same manner and in the same way as the next student. In a study, older students had an edge over younger students with decision making, understanding the concepts of learning in multiple ways and independent learning[xii]. Different subjects place different demands on different parts of your brain: Some school subjects involve creativity; others require problem solving; and many may require strong lungs like in a music voice class.

They say the first thing to go with age is memory. And I have to agree, except you can, and will have to, defy the symptoms of aging because some classes will depend on it.

Read the assigned homework on schedule. Oftentimes, it's dreadfully boring, but read it anyway. While reading, use a highlighting marker—orange, my personal favorite—for aging eyes. Then review the highlighted portion only at least every two days. Read it, read it again, and read it some more until you're nearly ready to drop out of school. At that time, you'll know you're on the right track.

Also, learn to speed read. Most professors assign an unrealistic amount of reading homework, especially for non-traditional students who most likely have a family to care for. The trick with speed-reading is to set a faster pace than you're used to. Then roll your eyes over the pages. Your brain will absorb at least 80 percent of the material. Well—it should.

Cliff's Notes are a no brainer for students who simply don't have time to read encyclopedias. These "notes"—which are really books with a yellow paperback—are summaries of a particular book. Not every book is summarized via Cliff's Notes, though, but the popular ones are. These books can also help you clarify information if you're having a hard time understanding the text. Reading is all about comprehension. And if you can't comprehend the material, you haven't read it.

At least one week before a quiz or an exam, create a hand- or type-written study sheet. Writing things down can help the information absorb into your brain. To go one step further, get a voice recorder and read off your notes to listen to it when you're getting ready for school. You can even listen to it in the car, at the grocery store, and talking to your mom while she's blabbering on about Uncle Chester's jigsaw-puzzle collection.

For list items, associate a particular word or phrase to something you're familiar with. To illustrate, for my geology class, I had to remember a list of rocks that only geologists had ever heard of, and I never wanted to hear of again. A partial list: Scoria, Slate, Gneiss and Pegmatite. The volcanic rock Scoria looks like a scouring pad, the thing people scrub pots-and-pans with. So I thought of that when I read the name on the exam: Scoria equals scouring. Slate is what homeowners use on the sides of their homes. Gneiss was tricky. But Gneiss looked "nice" because the rock looks like a zebra with multi-color banding. I thought that was "nice" a rock could do that... Nice it was! I stared at the Pegmatite rock for a while. How could I associate this word with something that was familiar to me?... Wait a minute; the rock was "pinkish" in color... "Pig!" Pigs are pink—Pegmatite. Pig—Peg—there it was.

For short-list items surrounding by lots of reading, acronyms and story creations with the first letter of each word works wonders. Using the same list—Scoria, Slate, Gneiss and Pegmatite—I've come up with two sentences with the first letter of each word: **S**ome **P**rofessors **G**rade **S**tudents or **S**illy **S**ally **G**ot **P**unched! Acronyms can be a little fussier. I could only manage GPS (**G**lobal **P**ositioning **S**ystem), but then there's one "S" left out. Can you think of other acronyms?

SEARCH ENGINE DIVING

Search engines like Google.com is an asset for research papers. But my husband always said, "The error happens between the chair and the keyboard." In other words, a search engine is only as good as its user.

Use keywords only to get the most out of search results. For example, if you're looking for advances in geoengineering, search for *geoengineering* only, not *advances in geoengineering*. Want to know the habit of an igneous rock?— okay, not really. How about the roles of women in the 19th Century? Type: *role women century*. The tricky part is figuring out how the Web site's author used *19th*. Did he or she use numbers or letters? You can type in both variations—*19* or *nineteen*—or you can leave it out altogether to manually filter your results.

In your search window, you can also type in specific words, but your results may be limited. Say you have over 20,000 search results, which is monstrous, add another word for focus: *role women century workplace*. Genius! And for keywords synced together—a direct phrase—use quotes around it: *"women in workplace."* Search results will show these words exactly as you typed them.

Google can also act as a dictionary. Yep. It has a brain. Type in *define: Coquina*. Coquina, by the way, is a limestone, sedimentary rock composed of shells. Google it!

ESSAY WRITING

A longtime friend, who had decided to go back to college at 34, called me one day in sheer panic: "I have to write a 1200 word essay! I don't remember how to write an essay! How do you write an essay? I'm so screwed! I'm going to drop this class!"

"You can't drop the class; it's English 101 and it's required for your major," I assured her. "In fact, you can't take many other classes, including things like history and science, unless you take English 101."

I had written more essays in history classes than I had in English or journalism writing classes. I vowed to help her and I gave her a sneak peak of this, the essay-writing chapter, before it was published.

Writing an essay is a real situation in college. And unless you've been a secretary popping out letters and copy daily, you're going to feel like an extraterrestrial that had just settled upon planet Earth. It's a piece of work.

The first thing to do before writing any essay is to figure out what you're going to write about. Most likely, the professor will assign something or set parameters for your piece. Once you get the assignment, brainstorm for the particular points you'd like to make in your essay. Brainstorming doesn't have to be perfect. The idea is to get your mind going with fresh ideas. My favorite brainstorming technique is "the bubble." That way, you can get as sloppy as you want. For example, I'll start with one word in the center; usually the word is the subject. Then I'll branch out from there.

The subject is: Should homeless persons work for their food?

Within this bubble are all of the points I could think to make in the essay. But believe me, if I had scanned the scribbles (read: chicken scratch) as it were drawn in my notes, you wouldn't be able to read it.

Here's the outline technique, although I think this one is much harder because your thoughts would have to be more organized:

I. Homeless persons picking in garbage cans.

    A. Unhealthy.

        1. Diseases.

    B. Dangerous.

        1. Hazardous materials could cause physical harm like used needles, broken   glass, etc.

II. Get back into the workforce.

    A. Establish work ethic.

        1. Pride & self-esteem.

    B. Get off the streets.

        1. No handout, a helping hand.

You can also simply create a random list of individual words or phrases that comes to mind. This is called "free association." With the homeless theme, let's see how many words or phrases I can come up with from the top of my head: dirty clothing, lice in hair, bath, sleeping on the street, no job, no bills to pay, ultimate freedom, bicycle, cold weather, decent shoes, food, health, nutrition—that's it! Once you've completed your list, scratch out words that you don't want to write about or that simply don't make since. You can also combine this technique with the bubble.

A WORD ABOUT GRAMMAR

Grammatically correct sentences should find their way into everyone's term papers, but academic language is so 80s. This type of language can leave your essays stiff and inaccessible, even to your professors (okay, probably not them). It can be identified by complicated, polysyllable words when one- or two-syllable words will do. For instance: *During days of observance, a multitudinous of patrons procures countless, futile products.* Did your mind go smack when you read that? A simplified version would read: *During the holiday season, many shoppers buy scores of useless products.* Do you see the difference?

❂ Recommended Reading – *Painless Grammar* by Rebecca Elliott, Ph.D. – This book goes over the basic rules of grammar, in case you need to brush up on many of them. This book is certainly a mainstay on my bookshelf.

BUILDING THE ESSAY

There are four things to remember with essay writing: TEEP - **T**opic sentence, **E**xplanation, **E**xample and the **P**oint. Just string those sentences together. That's a paragraph. Then repeat, repeat, repeat. For example:

➔ *Topic Sentence*: Tutor.com is an asset to non-traditional students around the country.

➔ *Explanation (explain why or elaborate)*: Sometimes professors lecture at lighting speed force, which makes it harder for many students to keep up.

➜ *Example (Illustrate a personal or general example here or you can always explain further to substitute an example. Also, you have to cite your references. Most likely with MLA (Modern Language Association formatting)*: That's because they have to pick a median speed they feel works for all students (Hartel, 6-7). Even still, this speed is to swift for many students like me.

➜ *The Point* (reinforces what you've written before it. It's the "Frankly, why should I give a damn?!" It is your thesis statement): Tutor.com can bridge the gap for all lagging students.

✪ *The point or thesis statement lets your professor know what your essay will be about, the point you will be making throughout.*

YOUR MASTERPIECE

Tutor.com is an asset to non-traditional students around the country. Sometimes professors lecture at lighting speed force, which makes it harder for many students to keep up. That's because teachers have to pick a median speed they feel works for all students (Hartel, 6-7)[3]. *Even still, this speed is to swift for many students like me. Tutor.com can bridge the gap for all lagging students.*

Bravo!

✪ Warning – Some professors loathe contractions like "that's (that is)," "haven't (have not)," "isn't (is not)," etc., so get the ground rules beforehand. Note that "its" is not a contraction. It is a possessive pronoun that shows ownership. For example: *The dog sat on its bed.* If you are unsure of what your professor wants, don't use contractions at all. Why risk it?

---

[3] MLA in text citation.

MORE ABOUT MODERN LANGUAGE ASSOCIATION (MLA) STYLE GUIDE

In-text citations add creditability to your essays and research papers. It consists of the author's last name of the book or article, and the page number, where you cited your information: (Hartel, 6-7). As you can see, the citation should be in parenthesis at the end of the sentence or a body of text. Plus, with citations, you'll need to back up any said claims in your manuscript—like when I was trying to prove that William Shakespeare's writings were complicated to read, to not just me.

I've inserted an introductory excerpt from one of my college papers. Note that the reference includes the author's last name and the page number:

Many students have read William Shakespeare's work and acknowledge his contribution to the literary arts—a cosmic genius of sorts—but undoubtedly, several readers criticize that his writings are difficult to read. In fact, he purposely complicated the English language to reveal a more poetic prose to mystify and captivate his audience. Strange lines of text embedded his poems, which were often not complete sentences, or he switched words around that made the sentences grammatically deficient by any collegiate standards (Shakespeare, XVII). Yet, he bore the creative license that allowed him to bend the rules. ...

Let's look at that paragraph again to analyze the TEEP structure:

Topic Sentence:

Many students have read William Shakespeare's work and acknowledge his contribution to the literary arts—a cosmic genius of sorts—but undoubtedly, several readers criticize that his writings are difficult to read.

Explanation:

In fact, he purposely complicated the English language to reveal a more poetic prose to mystify and captivate his audience.

Example:

Strange lines of text embedded his poems, which were often not complete sentences, or he switched words around that made the sentences grammatically deficient by any collegiate standards (Shakespeare, XVII).

[The] Point:

Yet, he bore the creative license that allowed him to bend the rules.

...

You'll have to create a separate page for all citations, books, magazines and Web sites that you referred to when doing research. It's called the "works cited" or "reference" page. You will start with the author's last name, which should be listed in alphabetical order with the rest of the references. Here's what your page will look like:

Works Cited

Doe, Jane M. "Title of an Article." <u>Title of a Magazine</u> 12 Sept. 1995: 53.

Lastname, Firstname. <u>Title of Book</u>. City: Publisher, year.

Lastname, Firstname2. "Title of Web site." 22 June 2007[*]. Owner of Web site. 30 Sept. 2004[**]

<http://www.markushartel.com/blog/about/street-photography-faq.html>.

---

[*] Date visited
[**] Date created

Public, John Q. "Title of an Article." <u>Title of a Scholarly Journal</u> 24 (2004): 119-25.

I've inserted a few more examples of essays and response papers I've written for classes. A response paper is a little different than a traditional essay because the professor wants your *response* to a particular written or visual work. Basically, you have to summarize the author's work and throw in your feelings wherever you can. Professors do this to make sure you have read the assigned homework.

The following response paper was written for a philosophy class, talk about screwing with your head. This class had me wondering if there was actually a chair beside me or if it was all in my imagination. The phrase went something like: "Does a chair exist in a room if no one is present?" "Does a tree in the forest make a sound if no one is there to hear it?"—*ugh*, okay. Moving on.

<u>WHAT IS JUSTICE?</u>

Irrational thought and lack of reason easily persuaded humans, which is why Plato rejected democracy as a form of the "ideal" government. His belief was based on the trial and death of Socrates, his mentor. The wisest and most enlightened persons—those who have acquired virtue and education—should rule a society. The rest, workers and guardians, should perform their unique duties, working together harmoniously, which would create a "just" state.

On the other hand, Aristotle, Plato's student, had a different view of human nature. He believed that men were political creatures by nature and existing in social communities only made them thrive, though he did agree that each human had their individual functions in society, as Plato did. But his take on justice was more even heeled: retributive justice dealt with how society should treat those who broke the law, and distributive justice dealt with how the distribution of wealth should be accomplished. ...

Notice that there are no citations in the aforementioned work. This is all from one book. In this case, a textbook. Usually, citations are not needed if everyone in the class is writing a response paper from the same book. With an essay, cite your sources anyway.

This next one is a smackamame doozy! This essay is from a geology class. Look at how the MLA style is implemented and the organization of thoughts. I had to research the heck out of this one!

Global-Warming Fix with Geoengineering?

An *Inconvenient Truth*, a documentary-film exposé starring Ex-Vice President Al Gore, sparked a resurgence of the global warming debate, though the debate is not a new one. According to an Intergovernmental Panel on Climate Change 1995 report, energy use has grown by two percent per year for almost the past two centuries. Rate reduction would require countries to radically halve their greenhouse gas emissions. Scatterbrained scientists have been moved to come up with radical solutions.

The burning of fossil fuels has increased with a 25 percent concentration of greenhouse gases in the atmosphere since the beginning of the Industrial Revolution (Flanagan, 34). To resolve some of the problem, the National Academy of Sciences (NAS) suggested sending 110 mirrors, 100 square kilometers in size, into orbit to reduce the amount of solar energy reaching the Earth's surface. This project comes with a hefty price tag of $120 billion. A similar proposal scheme would use a 2,000 kilometer wide solar reflector built from moon materials—placed 1.5 million miles from Earth—which would deflect two percent of the sun's radiation (Monastersky). Moreover, a parallel position would be to increase the reflectivity of the ocean's surface by film dumping with foams and white polystyrene chips into the oceans. Alternatively, this would create a "floating continent," made of white plastic (Flanagan).

No matter how worthwhile the abovementioned proposals seem, none of them are close to execution. But sulfur-dioxide injection into the stratosphere is under serious consideration. The process would mimic volcanic conditions, with the droplets acting like parasols, which would scatter solar energy (Flanagan). ...

WORKS CITED

Flanagan, Ruth. "Engineering a Cooler Planet." Earth Oct 1996: Vol. 5 Issue 5, p34, 6p, 6c.

Monastersky, R. "Can Science Whip up a Salve for Global Wounds?" Science News 30 Sept. 1995: Vol. 148, Issue 14, p222, 4/9p

National Academy of Sciences, Policy Implications of Greenhouse Warming: Mitigation, Adaptation, and the Science Base. Washington, D.C.: National Academy Press, 1992

The more experienced you get with writing an academic essay (hopefully, not dreadfully boring), you can mix things up a bit, but not too much because these rules are there for a reason, to create clarity and because they work!

Even if most students can live with writing an essay, most students would rather write another essay before editing one. Editing is a part of writing. It's like throwing your laundry in the washer, removing them and folding them into the chest drawer while still wet. You wouldn't think of doing that.

Looking over your essays at least once is a sure fire way to boost your grade.

At minimum, let your essay sit for at least one hour. In the best scenario, let it "cure" for twenty-four hours. No one can see his or her mistakes easily before that. Then, read it out loud, slowly. If someone else is in the room and you don't want to feel like an idiot, warn them first.

STUFF YOU SHOULDN'T DO, BUT WORTH MENTIONING

Plagiarism is dumb. Surely if caught, one could face class failure, or worse, expulsion from school. But what if you "recycle" your blood-sweat-and-tears research paper for another class?—with a little tweaking of course. Is it plagiarism or working smarter, not harder? I've never had the guts to ask a professor this, for fear they'd be on the lookout for my masterpieces.

Yet, many students do this, but no one would admit to doing it. Unless, of course, you're willing to buy them a beer and sneak a Cuban cigar through the border. Logically speaking, throwing it out would be a good waste of research, not to mention shaving a truckload of time out of your already strained days.

Even if you decide not to re-use your papers, you can always use the ideas for future research, so you don't have to go sifting through the school's library, again. Tip: save all of your files.

THE OTHER NIGHTMARE: MATH

You have probably forgotten how to do algebraic equations. That $x+7=10$ horror show? Obviously, the answer is 3. I spent most of my time in algebra class passing notes to one of the students sitting next to me.

Here is the correct way to "show your work," which is what your dreadful math professor will want:

Cracking the Gobbledygook!

- You want to solve for X because "X" is unknown. So what is it?

Take whatever is on the same side of the equal sign as X, which is "7," shown in *Fig. 1*, and subtract it by its opposite. The opposite of "7" is "-7." And +7-7 equals 0; they cancel each other out. Next, subtract that same number from the numeral on the other side of the equal sign. Do the rest of your calculations.

Solve for X:

Fig. 1

$$x-7=10$$
$$\underline{-7\ -7}$$
$$0\quad 3$$

$$\frac{x=3}{1\quad 1}$$

$$x = 3$$

- Bring the remaining calculations down, shown by the arrows: "X" equals "3." *Then*, divide the "3"––or whatever number is on the other side of the equal sign—by the "coefficient" of "X." Coefficient, you say, what in the hullabaloo is that? The coefficient is the number placed before the letter variable, the "X" in this illustration. There's no number there, right? Well, no and yes. Clearly, there is no number there. Anyone with 20/40 vision can see that. But in algebra, if no number represents the "x," there is ALWAYS a "1" in front of it. And "x" itself is "1" too. This rule looped me into a tree when I encountered it the second time around, although it had been too long ago to remember it the first go 'round.

- Take whatever is on the same side of the equal sign as X, which is "7," shown in *Fig. 1*, and subtract it by its opposite. The opposite of "7" is "-7." And +7-7 equals 0; they cancel each other out. Next, subtract that same number from the numeral on the other side of the equal sign. Do the rest of your calculations.

Fig. 2

$$x-2+7=10$$
$$\underline{+2\ +2}$$
$$x+7=12$$
$$\underline{-7\ -7}$$
$$x = 5$$

$$x = 5$$

Fig. 2 shows a more complicated version, with more steps, to jiggle your brain a bit. Now practice.

☐ I recommend *Cliff's Notes: Algebra I* as a stellar review guide for us ancient folks. Also, see "Recommended Readings" at the back of this book for more reference.

The examples presented are just to get your feet wet with algebra, again. I haven't covered multiplication, division, lowest common factors, square roots, trinomials (eek!) and a host of other mathematical problems.

The Cliff's Notes Algebra I guide will explain them all in detail. I am no math wizard—I'll save that for the math experts—but most likely, you will have to take at least one math class to earn your degree.

POINTS TO REMEMBER

- Learning how to learn requires the ability to change, and knowing that everyone's learning-capacity level is different.

- Reading the assigned homework is critical. This can lead to a better understanding of the material. Plus, the professor will reinforce this material through classroom lecture.

- All college students can't wing an essay like an academic scholar. Writing takes practice to become great at it. And it takes editing to get it near perfection.

- Plagiarism is dumb. Period. If caught, you could be expelled from school.

- Do I really need to talk about algebra?

9 THE 15 COMMANDMENTS OF CLASSROOM ETIQUETTE

There is a certain way to behave at the office, at your neighbor's barbecue, at church and in the classroom. I shall call it: "Classroom Etiquette." These unwritten rules of the classroom ensure a favorable learning environment for all students.

1. Who's older and wiser? You and your professors will most likely be a few years apart, with you being older. In all probability, the situation will be demeaning at first, but oftentimes, you'll find a good friend in him or her. Use these circumstances to your advantage. They could clue you in on "surprise" quizzes or throw some extra credit your way if you're not doing too well in class. But by no means should you date a professor, single or otherwise. It's unprofessional for them to do so and the people upstairs could reprimand them for it.

2. Far-fetched ideas in a far-fetched world: Sometimes, you will hear things in class that will make the hairs on your nape stand at attention, the professor slipping in a life lesson or has veered from the "truth" path. It's called preaching (Nope, you're not in Sunday school). They can't help it because their graduate degrees have given them license.

    It's okay to raise your hand and disagree, though not in a patronizing way. Respectfully. For example: "Excuse me your royal highness—" Let's start over: "Pardon me professor, I've read or heard that *this*, *this*, and *this* were more effective ways of handling it, sir/ma'am." Saying "sir," "ma'am" or "professor" will let them know you recognize their honorable status as authority figures, but you're respectfully disagreeing with them. If they have an ounce of dignity, they might even respect you for it. However, which can also happen, they would clamor through their desks for a yardstick and clobber you with it!

3. Raise your hand when you want to speak, but don't speak all the time. Give the other students a chance to shine. The last thing you want is a frothing-at-the-mouth young adult miffed at you for your know-it-all behavior. Extend them some courtesy or they can make your life a living hell.

4. Class participation is somewhere around 10 percent of the grade. Professors want you to ask questions, and look puzzled from time to time. The trick is obviously to have read the material beforehand. You can't participate if all you did last night was flop yourself in front of the telly. So if you're the shy type, it's time to pull a Kenny Rogers or Diana Ross recital in front of the mirror at least two months in advance. A fiddle or an Afro wig is optional. But getting the maximum effect to rid your shyness is your goal.

5. Seating location is prime real estate. Move your feet, lose your seat doesn't apply here. It's an un-written rule that where you sit on the first day, you've tagged it. That's your seat for the remainder of the semester. I haven't figured out why this weird phenomenon happens, although I have fallen victim to stool theft.

   a. Four sections exist in a classroom: the front (translation: near the professor), the back (as far away from the professor as possible), the window seat (*Did I put enough money in the meter?*) and the doorway (*Is he finished? 'Cause I'm going to be the first one out of here!*).

      Professors tend to play favoritism to those who sit in the front. They are very *serious* about their education. And these students deserve "A's," *wink*. As you can imagine, back-seaters are the scum of the earth. You and I both know that if you show up late, you're doomed to the bottom-dwelling heathens. The professors don't see it that way, although they'd tell you otherwise.

      The door area is the line of fire. Tardy students stroll in up until twenty minutes before the class is over. They've missed lecture; they haven't turned in their homework assignments; and they don't know what's due next week. Let's take a moment of silence for the death of their satisfactory grades...

6. Alcoholic beverages are not allowed anywhere on the campus grounds. That includes beer. Try not to sneak any into your coffee mug either (they know about that one too). If you're caught, you could be expelled, which would put you back to square one: a college dropout.

7. Cell-phone talking during class is downright rude. Tell your cardiologist you'll call her back. Even if the kids call, let the voice mail get it. They'll learn to share the remote control and take turns watching their favorite cartoons.

8. You shouldn't fall asleep during class. I know, I know, 18th Century literature isn't exactly a motivating wake up call. I've watched some of my "peers" sit at their desks with their eyes closed, a gapping hole in their faces, while snorkeling sounds detonated from their mouths. The trick is to master sleeping with your eyes open. Remember daydreaming?

9. Professors hate it when students are tardy—although they exempt themselves from this decree—because it's disruptive to the class and it hurts their egos. Set your clock and watches to college time. "Real" time isn't good enough, whether their time is off by, oh say, five minutes, ten minutes, none of that matters in college. I've known professors who rattled off with lecture for 15 minutes after the class was officially over. I know you really want to listen, but art history is waiting for you to do an analytical presentation on the color-choice palettes of Jackson Pollack.

10. Dust off the attic of your brain because college kids love to talk politics. Where else would they share all of that useless knowledge? The good thing about this is that you were probably alive when John F. Kennedy was president. The bad news is, with age, your memory is the first to go.

11. Spouting off about your favorite song or recording artist from the 60s, 70s or 80s is probably not a good idea. These students don't know the Mary Jane Girls from The Bee Gees. Now if you mention Hip-Hop Artist Ludacris or Justin Timberlake, you might get some buzz.

12. No matter how tempted you are to use the slang of your fellow budding students, don't. They'll recognize you as a fraud; you want to sound hip. Guess what? They don't use that word anymore. It's been thwarted off along with the words "groovy" and "ya dig?" Although the word "awesome" has been spotted from time to time like a Vegas-style Elvis.

13. You don't like it when someone preaches to your choir, so avoid the Reverend Sal E. Who role. The last thing you'd want to do is remind the other students of their parents. This will get you a first-class ticket to ostracism. The semesters can be long, so fight the urge to lecture them. Yes. Even when they do something stupid in your presence.

14. Don't squeal on the students too much. You'll be pegged as a tattle-tell. College kids still play this game.

15. Sexual harassment is not tolerated. Period. Probably back in your day, telling a woman, or man, how attractive she or he was in a hot outfit was acceptable. Grabbing them on the shoulder and *showing* them how hot they were in those garments is a sure fire way to get yourself into some deep dodo. Also, be careful using the words "suga," "sweet-heart" or "darling." These are words of endearment, something you'd call a loved one, not a stranger, let alone a professor or fellow student

In a Dzied and Weiner report study, 30 percent of undergraduate female students experienced sexual harassment from at least one of their professors. Schools that had no sexual harassment policy seemed to have higher incidences of harassment and had no training program for staff and students.[xiii]

POINTS TO REMEMBER

- Don't feel queasy if you're older than your professor. He or she still deserves respect. Besides, they have the power. You don't.

- Raise your hand if you want to contribute to a discussion or ask a question. Yes, you're still in kindergarten.

- Class participation is most likely part of the grade. If you're shy, tell your professor, so you both can arrange something. No professor wants a dead class.

- Find yourself a seat from day one and try to stick with it.

- Alcohol is not allowed on the school grounds. Period.

- Tardiness is disrespectful to your professor and the class.

- Try not to preach to the other students. They are not your children!

- Sexual harassment is dead.

10 DON'T PANIC! OKAY, MAYBE A LITTLE

THE FEAR OF FAILURE

Oftentimes, professors assign students into groups. It's usually the people sitting next to you, so there will be no awkward, oddball stances about who wants to team up with the "old" person.

With that in mind, from day one, sit next to someone who doesn't look too creepy; who looks like they bathe and do their homework assignments. To ward off your weird factor, you might want to wear the unscented version of Bengay, don't want rumors spreading.

Also, you will become a default team leader, and the mother or father figure whether you like it or not when you're working in groups. But heh, you're the ol' gal or guy and they will respect your opinion. But mostly, the fear of failure will be clawing into your backside. Surely, you'll channel that fear into diligence. The worst that could happen is the professor sends you into the corner for a time-out session while your ego gets tarnished. But college is not a place to buff your ego. Most likely, you will fail a class or two and get embarrassed from time to time. Ancient is as ancient does. With preparation, you can get through it without feeling like you just barfed all over your mother-in-law.

If you don't want to work in groups with your schoolmates, present your concerns to your professors beforehand. He or she may understand. Sometimes it takes the youngins a little while longer to grasp on to what the term "responsibility" is all about.

To make your anxieties worst, most of the younger students will be years ahead of you with academic knowledge. They'll make you wish you had paid attention in that high school, trigonometry class. But it's not to late to start again now. Use all of the resources the college and professor gives you. For example, don't try to save face during an exam. Use all of the allocated time. It'll feel like the pressure is on when all of your fellow students mosey out the door when it's just you left in the classroom. Hey, but if you're going down, you might as well go down yanking out somebody's toupee!

Hypothetically speaking, if you do manage to fail, get to know some of your peers so you can schedule classes together. Ever heard that misery loves company? It does. You and your peers can pass together and you can fail together. Networking also keeps you in the loop when missing class days, because you'll miss a lot. Not only that, the syllabus could change without warning (yes, some professors are actually that unorganized). You could wallop in one day—like a lackluster star on American Idol—on an exam. This buddy system is encouraging, but it can also score you some trouble.

Gaining friends at school makes for a smooth transition and plunge your remaining semesters full-speed ahead. But if you pass an exam and they plummet with an "F," you could lose them. Perhaps you both had made a pact that if you both failed a class, you'd repeat those classes together. You're not exactly keeping your end of the bargain, are you?

No two people learn in the exact same way, especially if there's a generation gap between you. The remedy: Try not to toot your horn too much; you can mix up the margaritas when you get home. And when your buddy asks you what you got on the exam, simply say, "I passed—but wow—I'm kinda shocked about it." No one wants to be second best.

In any event, drop a course if it's dead weight. Think of it: You have four classes. You're passing three, but failing one. You could try harder, pulling your other grades down, or drop one and get good grades in the others. You can always pick up the dropped course later. You can drop or withdraw from a course if you know you're failing within the first two to three weeks, or even up to two months. In the earlier scenario, you can drop the course without the incident that it might appear on your transcript. In the later scenario, a "W" grade will show the world how much of a quitter you are.

Dropping courses could also affect a student's financial aid—which could take you from full-time to part-time—so check with the financial aid department before you get trigger-happy. Don't worry too much about failing a class. Most colleges will give you an "R" grade—repeat—instead of an "F" grade—fail. Why? Because they don't want you to lose ~~their~~ your financial aid money. A college is still a business and you are their ~~customers~~ students.

SOCIALIZATION ANXIETY ATTACKS

It may be hard to make friends, not necessarily because of your age. Well, okay, that too, but because you may not have much in common with your young cohorts. You could be spouting off about the new Medicare plan that congress is debating, and your fellow comrades will only be interested in the latest pop CD release. The good news is that one-fourth of all college students are over the age of 30.[xiv] Non-traditional students tend to flock together like Feral Rock Pigeons on an acid-ruined building. Moral support has been an unscientific—dreamt up by Hartel & Company—determining factor. Both of you can share notes the new Medicare plan or your killer Roth IRA accounts. But be careful, non-traditional students probably know as much as you do.

Other things you have to worry about, college kids are not as open-minded and tolerant as you might think. If you've been communicating with only your neighbors for the past 10 years, and you both vote Republican, you might want to avoid sharing your personal views with your classmates. Sure, some college kids believe in drugs, partying and slacking off, but anyone who thinks differently than they do—as in the real world—they might be censored or shunned. Granted, most likely you will think differently than they do because you are from a different generation. If you are in a group setting or even in the classroom, share your opinion at your own risk.

THE ENVIRONS AROUND YOU

CLASSROOM MATTER

- Despite what might seem like the case, a college or university is not a professional environment. College can prepare its students—and potential students—for a lot of things. But certainly, it's no breeding ground for proper etiquette and practical solutions for everyday woes. The students talk during professors' lectures. Cell phones ring. Text messaging is conducted right next to you. *Sigh.* Keep in mind that those college students are not your children. Keep in mind that they could be.

- There's no good way to say this, but some professors are out-and-out weird. They come with their own luggage, just as you do. The higher-ups know about this phenomenon, but it seems that the more eccentric the professors are, the more "cultural" diversity they seem to have—at least that's what they assume.

- The professors are so used to dealing with young pupils that their teaching styles may be one-size-fits-all. So when they start yelling, it's not directed at you personally; if in fact they are indeed yelling at someone else.

SAFETY

- College is not a promise land where thieving crooks are dead bolted out. Crooks are everywhere, even in college. So never leave your valuable belongings unattended in a classroom. This goes for books too. Books are pricey. A crook could get a fair price for those, especially $100 textbooks.

- Fire drills are nearly non-existent at some colleges, so you'll need to devise a plan of your own. During the first week of class, plan your escape. Seek exit routes for each one of your classes and do this every semester.

    If you're a disabled student, especially in a wheel chair, find out the college's plan of attack if a fire or other hazard breaks out. In a fire, elevators will be of no use, and highly discouraged because a power failure could occur. If your class is on the top floor, you don't want to count on the kindness of your fellow student to carry you down nine flights of stairs.

= Personal Anecdote =

The 11 o'clock morning was brisk. *History of Western Civilization* class had just gained momentum when sirens rang on the fourth floor.

"What's that sound?" one of the students shouted.

The professor, scrawling on the chalkboard, turned around. "*Humpf.* I don't know. Sounds like a fire alarm." She continued scribing.

"Don't you think we should leave the building?" I asked, as I watched students herd down the hallway through the glass pane on the door.

The professor turned again, and then peeked at the door. "Yeah, I guess we should," she said nonchalantly.

Students bolted from their seats and squeezed through the doorway three at a time, merging with the other students. Fernando, a disabled student in a wheel chair, sat puzzled up front.

"I guess we have ourselves a situation," I told him as I approached. "Com'on."

He rolled with me. We joined the other students in the hall who were scampering towards the front exit. I knew I couldn't carry him down four flights of stairs alone. But everyone else was too busy trying to save his or her own hides. So we stood. Together.

"Did the school ever inform you of what to do in a situation like this?" I asked.

"Not really," he responded, "they just said to stay near the elevator until someone comes to pick me up."

"Right."

--

The story continued, with me writing a news-article for the student newspaper about fire safety protocols. Hundreds of students ran towards the front exit, but it hadn't occurred to them to use a back exit. They didn't know where they were. So you should. If there were a real fire situation, several people could have been seriously injured. Even Fernando.

CLEANLINESS

- The bathrooms can be downright creepy. Lack of funds or a lack of respect for students could possibly be contributing factors. Don't be surprised if you develop a rash or an itch that won't go away. Or some lung ailment. The bathroom attendants make their rounds about once per week, or so it seems. Bring along your own anti-bacterial wipes and keep a stash of toilet paper in your bag. The bathroom situation could get sticky.

DRUGS? NOOOO!

- Drugs are on college campuses too. Yes, most schools know about them, although they'll deny it to the bloody-gore finish. When I went back to college, the kids simply did them out in the open, unafraid of the security cameras posted in the yard. I was always skittish to whip out an Advil bottle for a headache, peering over both my shoulders as if I possessed the hot product.

OTHER WOW MOMENTS

- Remember in high school biology class when students dissected frogs? Some colleges are now cutting up house pets. At my college, students were dissecting cats. So if you're a PETA gold card member, it's probably time to re-evaluate your situation.

- One of the mature students I researched for this book stated that he didn't expect the whacked-in-the-face "liberalism" in the classrooms. Porno was shown in one of his classes, for analytical reasons, of course. If this happens to you, just make sure they have popcorn and the lights are dim. Any questions?

HOME LIFE

- Going back to college means the end of your lazy Saturdays, parking yourself on the sofa with your spouse and watching Housewives re-runs. Get a DVR, because at some point, like after graduation, you'll be able to catch up on year's worth of stuff.

- Tackling too many classes at once; joining a campus organization that's robbing your time; and juggling home- and school-life is a sure fire way to send your life into chaos. So keep a to-do list and plan everything. If something doesn't fit into your schedule, try something that does, even if it means not doing it. Prioritize things in your life. An action plan is always better than an unplanned flip-out. Most schools have counselors, free of charge, if things get bad and you need to vent or seek advice. You could also use the gym at school or learn new yoga techniques. I hear Madonna is doing well with this.

- You can take a leave of absence if you have a home or job situation that warrants your time. But not too long, or else the school administration will make you take those entrance exams again! Some colleges allow up to two years of everywhere else but school. Be careful of how much time you take off if you choose this option. Returning to school can be a real drag after so much time off. Then again, you should know that better than anyone.

- Your spouse may become threatened by your new learning experience. They might feel like you're "moving on" without them. Or they might resent the fact that you "get" to follow your dream and they have to put theirs on hold until the cows come home. Reassure them of why you're getting a college education in the first place; it's for the entire family, not just you.

More than half of students with a 2.25 GPA in their first year of college dropped out, which made experts question students' preparedness. Another risk factor included that a larger percentage of the students—20 years of age and older—had children of their own.

HELP!

- Whenever you get confused about what to do or where to go in the school, go to "student services." Most colleges have a student services center that can help you with just about everything you need. It's like having your own concierge, but I doubt if you'll get free baseball tickets, though it's worth a shot anyway. Student services can set up tours to your potential college or even help you find housing if you're relocating. Check your chosen school's Web site for student services information.

- On campus, just because someone is a "specialist" or an "expert" or "counselor" doesn't mean they know an orange from a mango transformed into an apricot. Sometimes these people guess to try and look smart, or the rules have changed since they last inquired about a situation like yours. You are your best ally. And in the end, you are responsible. Never trust one person's word on anything. Use your common sense. Ask at least three staff members, and if two of those persons agree, scrutinize those answers further. Research it and check it out yourself. Go to the president's office if you have to (but only if you must!).

- Most colleges have organizations for disabled students too. Disabled students should let professors know about their disabilities, so he or she can make the proper arrangements. Sometimes you must have proof that you are in fact disabled, unless your disability is visible. Otherwise, the professor might not believe you. A dyslexic student in one of my classes failed algebra because she didn't tell the professor about her disability (I failed algebra the first go 'round anyway). The professors should know, unless they are the president of the disability organization at the college, of course.

- Free tutoring center—right! Okay, to be fair, most colleges have tutoring facilities on campus, technically speaking. However, you might have to fight hundreds of students to get the attention you so deserve. Oh, I don't know, there may be one tutor per 20 to 30 students at any given time. I suggest you get a study group together, consisting of your fellow classmates. Most likely, you will have grasped things that your peers hadn't caught on to. And they will know things that you couldn't wrap your head around. The library offers rooms to students for situations like this. But you can hold a study group in a café, on the school's lawn, or even at a bar (hold the third round of martinis please!). Just be sure to stay focused on the material.

- Computer—if you don't own one, you can use the one at school. Most professors want typed papers. This also means that you can use that ragged typewriter that you've had since its invention. But don't hesitate to get a computer because you'll also have to do research. Supposing you haven't gotten into this digital age yet. It's time to get that microchip twinkle in your eyes. Computers are the future—for now, at least—although they said the same thing about electronic typewriters.

- You'll also need an email address so your professor can invade your private life on Sunday afternoons. They'll remind you to do your homework; read extra chapters; or just plain annoy you (I'm kidding... I think). You can get a "free" email account on Web sites such as www.hotmail.com or www.gmail.com, my personal favorite.

- Most colleges have healthcare facilities on campus, with services ranging from vaccinations, gynecological care, and other pesky ailments that you'd like to get rid of. Or the school may issue health insurance to all students.

The premium is collected from students' fees, which can range up to $100 or more per semester. Ask about these services if you think you might need them. You're paying for them anyway.

- Your school library has all types of researching information that you may need for class. For free! Lexis-Nexis and all these other Web sites that you'd normally have to pay hundreds of dollars per month is at your fingertips. Seek the help of a librarian if you have to.

Library books also help a ton with class research papers. But if you're looking for Tom Clancy's new release, you're probing for gold-rush leftovers. These books can be ancient, more ancient than you—honest. Most college libraries don't have the budget like public libraries, unless you plan to attend Harvard.

POINTS TO REMEMBER

- Everyone, including you, makes mistakes. So don't have the fear of failure control you, you control it.

- Don't be afraid to ask your fellow students for help. You might actually learn something.

- Students fail classes. No one person is great at everything (except my husband), but that doesn't mean you will fail college. That does mean that you will have to repeat the course in order to graduate, and to remove the "F" or "R," repeat, from your transcript with your new grade.

- Drop a course if it's dead weight. You can always repeat it later.

- There is a lot of diversity in college, people from different cultures around the world. You don't have to like anyone, but you should try to be tolerant of other students as long as they respect your boundaries.

- Censorship is at the last place on Earth where you'd thought it would be—in college. Keep this in mind when you go spouting off to your peers that you voted the late Ronald Reagan into office. Or if you're pro-war or pro-life. Many college students—and some professors—don't like it when you think differently than they do.

- Crime happens on college campuses.

- Check for escape routes in case of a fire or other emergency. Many students don't know where the exits are. You should.

- Keep anti-bacterial wipes and napkins in your bag for bathroom trips.

- Student services is a student's best resource, in most cases.

- Triple check any information a college staff member tells you. They could be wrong.

- Most colleges have a tutoring center. Don't be afraid to go there and don't be afraid to seek outside help if they're not helping (as in, too busy to help you).

- Don't forget to get an email address before you start college. This is very important. If you don't have a computer at home, go to your local library and set up one. If my mother can do it, so can you.

- Most colleges have free healthcare facilities for students, though I doubt if they can prescribe Viagra—contraceptives, yes.

- You can take a leave of absence from college if you must, but only, if you must, because we both know that it's going to be hard to get back into the swing of things.

11 GRADUATION: ARE YOU STILL ALIVE?

If you've made it to this point, pat yourself on the back, deservingly so, because you've just surpassed the unthinkable, surviving college as an older person. It wasn't easy, was it? Yahoo professors and laxer students who should've had a little more home-training when their parents unleashed them into the world. But it's over now! And now it's time to find a job. First, here's what to expect before you graduate.

HOW MANY CREDITS DO YOU NEED?

The secret about college is that it usually takes more than four years to graduate, five to six years is more like it. One-hundred twenty credits is the average required for graduation, but colleges sneak in more credits with prerequisites and things like language requirements that you hadn't factored in. Plus, many non-traditional students might have had to take remedial courses just to get back into the swing of things. These courses could range from reading, writing and one of my favorites—algebra—which could add an additional half-year to your load.

Don't forget, you have to actually file for graduation. The school doesn't keep track of your academic doings. Besides, they don't know if you're going to extend your stay, so you can work on twirling movements in that belly-dance class you may have just signed up for. Or you may repeat human anatomy so you can take another good look at your insides. As I've stressed before, in college, you are responsible for your own learning.

WHAT ARE YOU GOING TO WEAR TO GRADUATION?

Most likely, you will wear a dreadful robe over your couture garments, so wear comfortable clothing items. However, you, your family and friends might want to celebrate afterwards, so wear something you can feel proud of when looking back at those dreadful photographs.

THE GRADUATION EVENT IS NOT FREE

Colleges have to cover their expenses. They're a business and they can't eat the cost of the entire graduating class and their spectators—at least that's what their public relations persons would say. The best way to go about this is to have a plan: Will each members of your party pay their own tickets? Will you pay half? Or would you check into the Salvation Army's discretionary income about the tickets?

A FRIEND IN NEED IS A FRIEND INDEED

Be nice to your fellow graduates because they could end up being your boss. Not only that, networking in college is key. Most of the cushy jobs are not advertised. These jobs are also the least competitive. Why wouldn't they be? No one knows about them, except your college buddy who's got a killer job at an ad agency or at the local supermarket packing bags. But he knows about the position at the corporate office in the finely air-conditioned building. Still, a job is not promised to you. Hundreds, if not thousands, of people your age got their college degrees ten, fifteen, twenty years before you did. Although a college degree will increase your competitive edge in the job market, it will not promise you a job.

ARE YOU GOING TO GRADUATE SCHOOL?

Since you're in "school mode," you just might figure: "Why not go all the way?" You'd have a point. I thought about going to graduate school in my sophomore year. And had made a commitment to do so by the time I was a junior. But you're on your own with that information because those tidbits are in someone else's book!

THERE'S COLLEGE, THEN THERE'S THE REAL WORLD

You're up to date with all the internet gizmos and you start unloading all of your sexy pictures onto Myspace—*"I love you Pookey!"*—while using your real name and not a screen name. Dumb. You're employers know how to use Myspace and Facebook too. Leave those college tricks to the 19-year-old students. Your life will go on after college. Your internet profile is important.

LEAVING FRIENDS BEHIND

You've spent a lot of time in college, and as a human being, you've grown attached to the place. You've struggled with the other students, despite being several years their senior. You've created memories that hopefully won't last a lifetime, but your education will. Perhaps you've even created some life-long friends. And I don't dare say you'd like to repeat the experience. You can still keep in touch with the college friends of your choosing. That's a good thing, right?

POINTS TO REMEMBER

- Make sure you have enough credits to graduate. And make sure that you've met all the requirements that nobody told you about until the last minute.

- File for graduation. Sure, you've been at the college for the past few years, but they don't exactly *know* you.

12 THE [DREADFUL] WORKPLACE

INDENTURED SERVITUDE: INTERNSHIPS

Make sure to do internships starting in your junior year, earlier if possible. A prospective employer will want you to have experience in your newly chosen career, even if you've just graduated college. "How can I get experience if no one will hire me?" you might say. Easy. You can gain experience through school clubs and activities. You'll gain a heck of a lot of experience and pad your resume, to boot.

Sadly so, most internships are not paid. Experience or school credit is a form of payment. When a company doesn't have to pay you with money, they maximize your usage—indentured servant comes to mind. Luckily, internships only last about three months. Some last up to six months. It wouldn't be wise to sign up for this kind of servitude unless you're near graduation and you have a job hook-up there. But most college students have experienced this. If not, they should have. I've had five job references—via internships and school activities—by the time I was a junior. I had planned to do more by the time I graduated.

THE VANILLA RESUME

Two people could possibly interview you during a job interview. The other person may simply stare you up and down while the other person grills you, point by point, about your resume—which brings me to my next *point*: Bring two copies of your resume and cover letter.

Let your cover letter reflect your personal accomplishments, but don't mention you like to watch *Law & Order: Special Victims Unit* in your spare time.

This is way too personal. It's okay to mention the types of books you like to read or magazines (this makes you sound smart), but only if they are tasteful. You know the ones I'm talking about, underneath the bed?

Your resume may look like a clean sheet of paper with merely a name and address on top. You did do internships, didn't you? Include all of your previous internships and school activities on your resume as work experience. This can overshadow the fact that you're a newbie. Say, if you were the secretary of the bad-mitten club, include that. Or if you were the speaker of the student government, throw that in. Hopefully, you're not trumping up stuff from 1969; leave that out! Just make sure all of your accomplishments are there. You shouldn't even bother mentioning you were a homemaker or a college dropout in a different life on your resume. You can tell them in an interview, but only if they ask, and only if you must. Don't perjure or misrepresent yourself because an employer could verify that information easily.

Lynda Spiegel of Rising Star Resumes says that she's personally worked for companies where she was amongst one of the oldestemployees; "it seemed as though everyone was the same age as my ownchildren," she said. "Getting hired in that situation was pretty tough. Obviously, olderpeople can bring experience, patience and wisdom to a youthful culture, butthe stars have to be in alignment for you to convince the hiring manager ofthat."

A one-page resume is still ideal. Business people simply don't have time to read novel-length manuscripts about your life (and you certainly don't have the time). So make their lives easier, not to mention making it easier for you to get the job.

And, *Ugh*, don't type your resume and cover letter in fancy smancy, Lucinda Handwriting type fonts—or anything with "curly ques" for that matter. Courier and Times New Roman are professional looking fonts that are universally accepted and expected. These fonts show that you are at the top of your game, despite being a fresh graduate. They also show that you follow the rules. Employers are skittish about hiring people who they feel constantly change the "normal" order of business.

WHAT YOUR RESUME SHOULD LOOK LIKE

Make your resume list style, not essay style. This form will make your resume easier to scan quickly for the busy employer.

• **Here's what *not* to do:**

Essay Style

Jan. 2007-May 2007 - *Kingsman* newspaper: As a news and feature writer for the *Kingsman*, I was assigned stories each week for one or both sections. The news' section required the writing of events, student meetings and profiles of faculty and staff. The feature's section involved in-depth, investigative pieces and off-the-beaten-path news stories, which I often pitched.

• **Here's what to do:**

List Style

News and Feature Writer - Brooklyn College *Kingsman* Newspaper Jan. 2007-May 2007

- Wrote news stories on campus events and student meetings

- Profiled faculty and staff in articles

- Pitched stories to the managing and feature's editor

Do you see how easy the last one was to read? Not only that, each sentence began with a verb. Using a verb will get the resume reader in the right frame of mind.

Even still, sometimes that may not work. After at least 20 resume submissions and no takers, perhaps your lack of responses is not about your job skills; that is, if you're surely qualified. But perhaps it's the written tone of your cover letter. To illustrate, here is a cover letter that I had written to grab an internship. I had an editor look it over—which she really re-wrote—to smoothen out the rough edges:

Sabrina Hartel

123 E. 456 Street • New York, NY 54321

Tel. (212) 555-4321 • Fax (800) 555-1234

Email: sabrina.hartel@email.com

Cover Letter

As a journalism student at Brooklyn College, I have exposed myself to a broad range of what the industry has to offer, in the hopes of learning as much as possible about my chosen craft. While in school, I have contributed to the *Kingsman* student newspaper as a news and feature reporter; I also worked as a freelance intern reporter for the *Manhattan Times* and an editorial assistant intern for Manhattan Media, publishers of Quest, Avenue, West side Spirit and Our Town newspapers and magazines, just to name a few.

I've learned that diligence, dedication and hard work are demands that are expected of you in this field. I'm a team player and I'm not afraid to roll up my sleeves and go beyond the job description when called upon. I'm also not afraid to ask questions.

I hope that any opportunities you can offer me in the form of an internship would only help to broaden my capabilities and experience as a writer. Thank you so much for your time and consideration. I would greatly appreciate the chance to meet with you and discuss this opportunity at further length. My resume and writing samples are attached.

Sincerely,

Sabrina Hartel

This might look fine and dandy on the surface, but this cover letter stinks! Why? Because no one talks like that. Well, okay, maybe that lady on the Home Shopping Network, but not you. And you shouldn't. I got no takers with this travesty. It took me three months to realize that that cover letter was stiffer than an oxford shirt. I didn't know any better at the time. I thought, 'Heh, if a professional writes it, it must be golden. Right.

Then I toned it down with a more relaxed piece of text:

Sabrina Hartel

123 E. 456 Street • New York, NY 54321

Tel. (212) 555-4321 • Fax (800) 555-1234

Email: sabrina.hartel@email.com

About Me

I'm a journalism student at Brooklyn College and have interned at a handful of media companies. As an editorial-assistant intern for Manhattan Media (publishers of *Quest, Avenue, West side Spirit* and *Our Town* newspapers and magazines), for example, part of my job was to re-write press releases to fit into the newspaper's restricted space. During that period, I re-wrote nearly 100 press releases, which provided me with invaluable experience. I also took note of what my superior, the managing editor, did or did not like about each press release.

I'm a savvy researcher and familiar with AP style. My journalistic writing styles include hard news (inverted pyramid) as well as feature stories (events, profiles, human-interest, etc.). The goal is to convey information in an easy-to-read, yet entertaining news-release article.

Together with journalism, business marketing is my college minor, although it will play a major role within my career goals as a public relations professional. Marketing is not only about marketing products, but marketing ideas, services and persons.

I'm highly organized and take full use of an e-calendar and Post-it® Notes while administering office duties. I'm a team player and not afraid to roll up my sleeves and go beyond the job description when called upon. I'm also not afraid to ask questions.

I hope that any opportunities you can offer me in the form of a paid internship would only help to hone my capabilities and experience. Thank you so much for your time and consideration. My resume and writing samples are attached.

Sincerely,

Sabrina Hartel

This one worked and landed me a few other internships. It sounds less stiff, but still slightly fluffy in tone. After four or five internships, I didn't care whether someone gave me another one or not. I was on the verge of being overqualified. I browsed the job boards anyway and found a listing that peaked my interest. Here's the email I sent, making sure to use the right buzzwords that were listed in the job description:

Sabrina Hartel

123 E. 456 Street • New York, NY 54321

Tel. (212) 555-4321 • Fax (800) 555-1234

Email: sabrina.hartel@email.com

Lazy, absent-minded? Not me. Smart, driven and might I add efficient? Then you're talking my language!

I'm a hungry journalism student at Brooklyn College who's wrapped myself into media since my freshman year. Hard work is good for the soul and creativity? Well, a non-creative mind is a mind that hasn't reached its fullest potential—I won't bore you further with my accolades. My resume and writing samples are below.

Best regards,

Sabrina Hartel

I got a call from the company within one hour and seventeen minutes after shooting off this email. How's that for loose-lipped! I wouldn't recommend this level of pompousness if you actually needed the job or internship. But sometimes breaking the rules is necessary.

THE ~~INTERROGATION~~ *INTERVIEW*

You will spend nothing shy of a few hundred dollars for work-attire once you land a job. You'll need at least six outfits to mix and match; that's one outfit for five working days, and an emergency suit in case you didn't get laundry done over the weekend. A new pair of shoes is also in order. Buy something that matches all of your garments, like a neutral color. The last thing you'd want to do is show up at a job interview in your lavender wing tips!

I'm sure you've read how-to-do-well-on-a-job-interview articles in the local paper or a magazine. But here's the deal, being your *true* self is the way to go. If a company hires you, they'll find out who you are anyway. They can still fire you then. Save yourself the headache and fire the representative who would normally speak for you. This is not to say that if you normally roll out of bed without showering that you should do that on the day of a job interview. You can alter these tangential things. And even kick-start some new habits from here on out. But changing oneself from the inside takes several visits to a shrink.

When I was looking for an internship, I simply wanted a job that paid. And the one I was interviewing for, at the time, did. But when the interviewer asked me, "Why this job? Why this field?" I couldn't give her a real answer. Then it struck me: I didn't want to work in *that* particular field. I found it extremely boring! I just couldn't let her in on the fact I had my eye on a new pair of sling-backs.

But if you must have that job, saying the right things could get you there. When an interviewer asks you why you want that job, instead of saying, "Money!" say, "I'm seeking more career opportunities." If it's a career change, say, "I'm finally seeking my life passion, my life calling." Instead of saying, "I need a job!" say, "I know this is what I've always wanted to do as soon as I started college." To really impress them, do background research on the company and add in specifics: "This company has been the leader in real estate for the past seven years, especially now with the merging of XYZ Corporation two years ago." They'll respond on the inside: 'Wow! This bozo has done his or her homework.'

Art Koff, founder of RetiredBrains.com, chimed in with some verbal exercises that could clear your pipes and send the right message:

Present yourself with concrete examples of your role and accomplishments.

What was your role, title, team type and position within the team?

Examples of how to do so:

"As Director of _____I...."

"I was responsible for..."

"As a member of the product team..."

"When I taught or instructed I..."

What did you do?"

I created, led, initiated, designed, developed, simplified, organized, facilitated..."

Examples:

"I developed a plan that ..."

"I created a process that..."

"I led the team that..."

What was the result of my efforts?

"I increased, improved, reduced, achieved..."

Examples:

"I reduced vacancy rates 30%"

"I improved test scores by 20%"

"I achieved highest-ever attendance levels"

"I increased call efficiency by 10% for 3 consecutive quarters."

Most importantly, be honest with yourself. Ask yourself some real questions and provide yourself with real answers. Is this the sort of thing you can see yourself doing for the next five years? Ten years? Believe it or not, jobs are plenty, as long as you have a flexible degree. So don't jump at the first job offer because they're offering money. They all are. Respect your intuition and don't be a rocket scientist unless your heart absolutely desires it.

= Personal Anecdote =

During the summer of my junior year, I cruised online job postings like I normally did. I emailed my resume left and right and got a few interviews, but no serious prospects. And to tell you the truth, I wasn't that impressed with the nuts-and-bolts many of them were offering, like no pay.

Later that day, I came across an interesting job post, with words like *"... elite company ... looking for dedicated, outgoing ... ,"* I'm there! I read on: *"...* marketing and public relations ... ,*"* I'm still following. They must be reading my resume through clairvoyance!

I immediately emailed them. Two minutes later, I received a reply: "Can you interview next week?" I answered: "Yes, I can interview next week." She bounced back: "Call this number and ask for Gina." Me again: "Okay."

I called the number. A woman answered and asked me if I had sent a resume. I told her about the email series and left the person's name. "Okay, let me check your resume and call you back in ten minutes," she said. I waited.

Ten minutes went by, and then the phone rang. "Sabrina Hartel," I answered.

"Hi, this is Gina getting back to you—"

"Okay."

"What year did you graduate high school?"

"May 2009."

"No. What year did you graduate *high school?*"

My voice crippled as I clamored through my wits. "*Ugh.* Let's see. 1993." I couldn't remember *exactly.*

"You know this internship is unpaid?"—translation: older people want money and we don't have any to give them.

"Oh really?"

"Yes."

"I'm sorry then. I was looking for a *paid* internship."

The conversation ended.

Employee interviewers can sometimes be downright weird. And their weirdness may exude in your presence in the form of an interview. Take a look at some of these oddball interview questions, reported by Glassdoor.com, along with some fresh answers that I rallied up:

Question: "If you woke up and had 2,000 unread emails and could only answer 300 of them, how would you choose which ones to answer?"

"I'd scan for any from friends or family, then from work associates and lastly blogs I subscribe to. If I had any room left after that, I'd pick some that came to my LinkedIn inbox as sometimes those are authors requesting an audit." - Carrie A. Aulenbacher, author http://www.carrieaulenbacher.com

"Let's start at the very beginning, a very good place to start..." I answer emails in the order received, since fair is fair." - Kirsten B. Feldman, author of NO ALLIGATORS IN SIGHT and ON THE WAY TO EVERYWHERE.

Question: Describe the color yellow to somebody who's blind.

"It's like getting a hug from someone you really care about. - Shantavia

"Have you ever sat in the sun and felt the light on your face? That's yellow.. Or perhaps have you listened to Vivaldi's The Four Seasons? "Spring" is yellow. Or, you know the feeling you get when you're out of school for the summer? That's yellow. Lemon tastes yellow, as does vanilla, though they are two different shades. Sour lemon is a bright, greenish yellow, while sweetened lemon is a medium, rich yellow, and vanilla is a very pale, creamy yellow." - Sophia Martin, author of the Veronica Barry mystery series and the Raud Grima fantasy trilogy on Amazon.

Question: Who would win a fight between Spiderman and Batman?

"It would be a blood bath cause they are even with powers. No one would walk away." - Brian T.

"Spiderman because he is stronger, faster and can shoot his spider web at Batman from a distance!" - Charles Cannon - http://www.charlescannon.com.

"Never got into super heroes. But I would think that Spidermanshould be able to tie up Batman in cobwebs and immobilize him in a wellstaged daytime attack- Assuming Batman like a bat is nocturnal." – Dr. Judi, http://www.drjudic.com

Question: If you were asked to unload a 747 full of jelly beans, what would youdo?"

"Ask how long my lunch break was. When the interviewer frowns, I'd follow upwith questions on available offloading hardware and staff, trucking &warehousing options, and ultimate disposition of said jellybeans todetermine short and long term strategies." – Don Stewart, MD – Chief Visual Humorist, The DS Art Studio Gallery in Birmingham.

Robert Nordlund, CEO of Association Reserves, asks his own questions: "We regularly ask, "What would I learn about you by taking a ride with you in your car?" Followed up by, "What's in your trunk?"

Jean Marie Dillon, a C-suite Human Resources professional, said, "If I were faced with any of these questions, I would answer: "Had I known that performing like a circus animal in a cage was a requirement of working at this company, I would have reconsidered my application." I would be curious to hear the interviewer's response to THIS answer."

That's all on that matter, folks.

Don't shoot yourself in the foot regarding salary. Salary history will follow your from day one. If you know the rock-bottom salary for your career profession—because you've done the research—is $45,000 per year, don't accept a job for $35,000. The base will most likely be your starting salary, so be choosy, not desperate. You've got a degree now. People will hire you—eventually.

GETTING AROUND TO THE AGE QUESTION

You don't have to tell your employer your age in a job interview. In fact, age discrimination is illegal. It's unlawful for an employer to specify age preferences in a job ad unless the age is a bona fide occupational qualification.

In 1967, Congress thought that employers who set arbitrary age limits—instead of on skill set—were performing an injustice to persons over 40 years old. This was also cutting into the federal government's tax revenue. So they made it illegal to do so with The Age Discrimination in Employment Act (ADEA). It's a win-win situation for you. You get to further your education and get a job no matter your age. But some cases still fall through the cracks.[xv]

Obviously, if you're sporting more gray hair than Ms. Clairol can handle, you're headed up a creek in a tugboat. Many employers feel that older employees want more money than they can offer, because you have real bills to pay. Also, sometimes an employer wants to mold you to fit into their scheme of things. If you have more mileage than a young buck, they might think that an old habit—or way of doing things—will be harder to break. An employer wants to know that your skills are newly packed and up to date. Do computers come to mind?

In the end, an employer will hire you if you fit into their program because all the degrees in the world cannot fit a square peg into a circle. This is a good thing and works both ways. You wouldn't want to work in an environment where you don't get along with any of your co-workers. You have to spend a lot of time with their weirdness. Ask your neighbors if they love their jobs. Then ask them why.

OFFICE POLITICS

What kind of company would you like to work for?—a large corporation, mid-size company or a boutique, family size business.

The right type of company will make all the difference of whether or not you feel like you're stuck in a cubicle with three walls and a bottomless pit as a floorboard. With large companies, each worker has its place, but the workers do nothing more than their assigned duties. For example, my husband works for a large corporation as a graphic artist. He beautifies all the fabulous models you see in the magazines; just a tip, they're not really skinny and they have lip hair, but that's beside the point. He's also a computer geek, so he can maneuver an Apple computer like a flying mantis. But if his email software glitches, he can't troubleshoot that on his own. It's not within his job description. That's for the IT (information technology) guys.

Some of you might say, "Great. The less work I have to do, the better." But for others, this boundful box may seem frustrating, especially if you have more than one skill. Your hands are tied, even if the task seems like a natural transition from your job description to the next—no can do. The upside is that large corporations tend to pay higher salaries. They have the dough to do so. They oftentimes have stockholders funding their capital. And merging with other companies tends to be commonplace, which could lead to layoffs.

Employers are apt to wearing many hats at small and mid-size companies. They don't have the financial resources to have it any other way. Administrators double as receptionists, mail clerks, bike messengers and Mr. Coffee. Employees in this work environment get to think outside of the box on many levels, which stretches job experience and skill set. They both tend to give out more job titles to over compensate for the measly salary they're paying their employees. However, red-tape enthusiasts and hierarchy buffs won't thrive in this environment because you actually have to work.

WORK ETHICS

People do strange things to get ahead, and oftentimes, will mash on anyone along the way to get there. This is what people do for money. Competition is fierce, even if there are only five of you in the office. Your fellow co-workers will rat you out if they *have* to. Don't do or say anything in front of them that you wouldn't do or say in front of your boss.

Browsing the web and checking your personal email account at work will certainly give your co-workers some ammunition. A stunt like this could land you into the unemployment's office. And no one should send—or have sent— –questionable emails to a corporate email account. Jokes, granddaughter photos and hijacked software should be sent via personal email, so you can check it at home because companies have access to this email account.

STILL NOT CONVINCED?

Still not convinced that you're ready to get out there or start a new career path? Here's some quick take-a-ways to push you out the nest:

1. Apply for jobs that you are actually qualified to do. This will save you time and not waste the recruiter's time. Not to mention, you'll keep a soft spot in the recruiter's heart for the future if you seek employment there once your resume has seen its fair share of miles. For example, if the position is seeking someone with 3 years of experience and you have 3 months of experience--an internship, to boot--not a good idea.

2. In relation to tip #1, get an internship in your chosen field if your resume looks like a clean sheet of paper. Not many employees like to hire someone with no experience. A 3 month internship, paid or unpaid, counts as experience.

3. Get a LinkedIn account set up. Many companies have recruiters on staff (or contract) to seek out potential employees, especially if the job needs to be filled fast. Not only that, you'll get to show them how nice of a smile you have vis-a-vis the selfie you took.

4. Be yourself on a job interview. The potential employer called you in for a reason, so you look good on paper. They want to see if you have chemistry. It's like going on a first date. The person on the other side of the table may look sweet or dapper in that silky blouse or crisp cotton shirt, but little did you know, they snore! Do you see how this could put a damper on things?

5. Your new job is to look for a job. Looking for a job is work, not a feat that's done between chores. Set a goal for how many resumes you'll send out for the day. When I'm between jobs, my goal is to wake up at 7am and send out at least 6 resumes for the day, everyday, which shortens my unemployment time to no longer than 2 months. Then I can go back to watching Jerry Springer.

POINTS TO REMEMBER

- Include all of your internships and school activities on your resume. This counts as experience.

- Don't write stiff and overly formal cover letters, because in real life, nobody writes like that (except scientist and academics). The purpose of this cover letter is to let you shine through.

- A one-page resume is more ideal than a 10 page epic saga, and stick with Courier or Times fonts. An Arial font is okay too, but do you want to show them that you like to break the rules that much?

- Create list-style resumes. They're easier to glance quickly.

- You don't have to reveal your age to an employer if you don't feel comfortable.

13 ADVICE FROM NONTRADITIONAL STUDENTS

So you don't have to go at it alone, I rallied up some nontraditional students and solicited advice from them. Here's what they had to say:

I started nursing school right before my 51st birthday for a two-year associates degree program. My advice:

1. The work will be easier than it was when you were a teen, because your focus is on education, not on your peers.

2. Don't try to "fit in" with the younger crowd, they won't let you and just when you think you have, someone will remind you that you don't.

3. You have so much more life experience than the younger ones; they may not believe all of your personal life stories or examples. (Or care for that matter).

4. If your instructor is around your own age, watch out for other students seeing you as getting "special treatment" even though there isn't any.

5. Remember that you have as much or more value to contribute to the classroom or profession as the younger students.

6. Don't trust anyone other than yourself when it comes to getting the work done.

7. Make sure your husband / family support your effort enough to understand why things aren't done the way they used to be. I could probably go on and on, but that's enough for now.

-- D. Turner, 55 yrs old, Richmond VA.

I went back to school at 40 - divorced and with 4 kids under 14. I would advise those brave souls to figure out what they are going to let go. Mine was housework. The new laundry plan was that if I could not see an actual stain or smell it at arms length, you could wear it again. And "dirty" took on a whole new meaning. The house was clean unless there was something toxic to remove. It was painful to lower my standards, but I have a 3.8 GPA.

-- Julia Angelen Joy Z Group PR, Inc. www.ZGroupPR.com

I was 33 years old and scared to death when I quit my job, sold our house and moved 1,000 miles to trade my AAS degree in on a BS degree. Less than 8months later, I was teaching electronics at the university I was attending. I ended up teaching electronics for 28 years. As a college instructor, I hadmany mature students.

-- Mark Hughes, author of The New Civil War Handbook
http://www.civilwarhandbook.com

In one situation where I had gone back to college at 35 I walked into the classroom and some of the younger, traditional students began asking me whether they needed their textbook that day and would the final exam wouldbe comprehensive.

Yeah. That was a bit embarrassing.

The few pieces of advice: 1. You have already been through hell raising your children; completing your degree is nothing. Your textbooks don't yell at you, don't have chores they didn't do, and don't require you to have sleepless nights waiting upfor them on their first date (or prom night).2. Time management is your only friend. You have a busy life; you must plan your days and weeks to fit in 200 hours in a week that only has 168 hours total.

This means you may only get 5 or 6 hours of sleep a night. There is a light at the end. Once you get that diploma--there are no words to express what you feel.

-- Montgomery Beyer, MBA

I returned to college after working 20 years and got my master's and subsequently my PhD. in Communication Studies. I now am on my second career as a college professor. One of the things that threw me upon returning to college was how term paper writing had changed. I went to school in the days of footnotes and bibliographies. I returned to school and they were talking about MLA and APA and I had no idea what they were discussing. I had to teach myself how to write research papers. No one told me about citation software that would do the bulk of the work for me, so I struggled needlessly because I was too proud to admit I didn't know what I was doing.

As a professor now, I see the benefits of being a non-traditional student. By and large, my non-traditional students have a deeper understanding of course material. Because they have life experience, they can relate to course materials and theories in a way that traditional students cannot. Those thinking of re-entering academia shouldn't be afraid of returning to school. All they need to remember is that fear and pride are the only two things that can hold them back. Their maturity and experiences make them better students. However, things have changed and admitting that you don't know something and asking for help is the secret to success.

-- Eilene Wollslager, PhD, APR

I am 40 year old student returning to school to finish up a degree in Graphic Design. The most surprising thing to me when I returned to school in 2013 was the teachers' ban on technology in the classroom. I thought for sure I would be able to use my iPad to record lectures or my laptop to take notes, butalmost every professor I had did not allow any use of technology for fear that students would use it to peruse social media during class instead of as a study tool. Of course, I looked at it like it's my tuition money paying their salary, so if I wanted to use class time to check my twitterfeed - as long as I am not disruptive - then that should be my choice!

-- Rachel HurleyChief EvangelistScrewpulp.com

I returned to college in my mid-thirties to obtain a Master's in Psychology. Personally, I took the experience more seriously than I did back in my twenties. I was more focused and organized. I was also keenly aware of how much money I was spending, which got me to turn off the TV and do my homework even when I didn't feel like it. Some of my life experiences did get in the way. I once wrote an essay on my meditation experience and got tagged for numerous spelling errors. The words weren't misspelled; they were Japanese and Chinese. The instructor was being lazy and letting MS Word spellcheck's English dictionary do his job for him. He was quite embarrassed when I pointed out this gaff to him. Samuel

-- MorningstarPrairie Village, KSSci-fi author

I was 50 when I went back to school. I received a BS in education in 1980; an MS when I was 33, an Ed.S. in school administration when I was 51, and an Ed.D. when I was 53. As I was finishing my dissertation, the schooldistrict downsized and I lost my job.I spent many years showing teachers, administrators, churches, and organizations how to define their purpose, align their vision and mission with their core values, and create tangible goals. I had to figure out how to that organizational goal-setting process and make it personal. That struggle led to my goal-setting workbook for individuals struggling to transform a dream into a plan of action, Dreams to Action Trailblazer'sGuide<http://amazon.com/Dreams-Action-Trailblazers-Guide-Connor/dp/0991487206>

-- ***Julie Connor, Ed.D. *www.DrJulieConnor.com**

I began a doctoral program at age 37 -- the same week I happily learned that I was pregnant with my fourth baby. Working full time as a school counselor, I drove 75 miles to the university one night a week and on Saturdays. I felt very lucky to have this schedule, but my luck ran out during the second semester when I went into labor on an early Saturday morning. My husband and I timed the contractions for a couple hours, and then I made a phone call. To the doctor? No. To my parents? No. My first call was to my professor. "I'm sorry that I won't be in class today, as I'll be busy giving birth, but I'll see you next weekend."

-- **Karen Gorback, Ph.D. – Karen wrote an article titled: "Headed for the Future – A Boomer's Guide to Returning to College" in the Spring 2014 Journal of Certified Senior Advisors, page 11. You can view it here:**

http://bit.ly/1zpq6Ow

While I did go back to graduate school as a non-traditional aged student, I do have some insight regarding older students entering undergraduate education. After 26 years of teaching college students, I've noticed that older, non-traditional students tend to be the better students. Their penchant for success is based on a number of criteria: greater self motivation to do their best, a personal financial investment in their education, a need for career advancement, and the desire to set an example for their children and grandchildren.Although driven to succeed and better prepared, I have also found that many of these students lack self confidence in their work – as they feel that gap of years between high school and college is a liability. Unfortunately, they do not realize that they are wiser due to their life experiences. Inmost areas they are better prepared than their traditionally aged peers. Older students usually soar to greater academic heights than they had in high school.

-- James M. Owston, EdD, Associate Professor of Mass Communication,Alderson Broaddus UniversityPhilippi, WV

I went back to school at age 35 with two kids and one on the way.Advice for non-traditional student:

1) Make sure you have good back -up systems. Without the back -up help ofmy parents and in-laws and friends it would have been hard to weather allthe crises big and small.

2) Never leave anything for the last minute. There appears to be a newMurphy's law especially for older students : if you leave something forthe last minute, the kitchen floods or the kids contract the chicken pox.

3) Invite three of four other older students to grab a quick lunch togetherso that you can build a support group. You need people with whom tocommiserate. Your family may not understand the environment and demands ofyour school.

4) Trust yourself,. You are alder now and better able to judge whatreadings are worth reading fully and completely and what readings are worthskimming.

5) Enjoy the privilege of being given a second chance. Previousgenerations and people in other parts of the world don't get theopportunity. Embrace every opportunity you can.

-- Ruth Nemzoff, author and speaker Don't Bite Your Tongue:* How to FosterRewarding Relationships with Your Adult Children* and Don't Roll YourEyes: Making In-Laws Into Family ,Brookline, MAwww.ruthnemzoff.com

I'm 49 and am in my second year of college. I never went when I was younger. I wish I had been more tech savvy before starting school. It seems like everything is online now. The library, all my professors communicate through emails and the school's website. I would say any older person wanting to go back to school learn to use computers if they don't already know how, they won't survive if they don't. I just recently found out that all textbooks I need can be purchased through my nook - all those heavy books I wouldn't have had to carry the last year!One tip I would give is to make sure one allows for plenty of study time. I work full time and had a heavy class load my first semester. I managed to pull a 4.0, but it took a lot of sleepless nights to do it! I was told by an advisor not to carry more than half credits, but no, I figured I was allowed up to 12 per semester and I could handle it. Boy was I wrong!One nice thing I did learn was that older students are not uncommon in this day and age. I felt funny the first couple of days - an "old lady" walking around campus with all the young kids - but those young kids not only didn't look at me funny, they were very helpful. Those that didn't mistake me for a professor anyway :)

-- Anonymous

I have been counseling students for over twenty years, many of whom are nontraditional.

It is important to emphasize the issue of confidence. Some of my students begin to doubt themselves as they get closer to matriculation. After all, they have been off the academic track and this is in many ways a return experience for them. Intellectually they know (and we discuss) the professional and worldly experiences that they bring to the classroom, but there is often some self-doubt that seeps in along the road back to school. I almost always point out the irony of this, given that returning nontraditional students tend to excel in school far beyond where they would have had they not taken time to clarify their goals and reflect on their educational objectives.

-- Steven Roy Goodman, MS, JD, Co-Author, College Admissions Together: It Takes a Family

I have a very unique story. I'm finishing my second year at HampshireCollege and I have just turned 28. I had planned on going to school mysenior year - I was your typical type A teen who had SAT tutoring weeklyand applied to 17 top-notch colleges. Two weeks after I had gotten mycollege acceptance letters, my stomach randomly exploded due to a bloodclot, fell into a coma, couldn't eat or drink for over three years, and adecade later (and 27 surgeries later) I'm fine now. But I always wanted acollege education, so at 25, I reapplied. It was strange getting back intothe "college game" - I even saw my old college counselor! I was surprisedto know that 10 years later, nobody cared about SAT scores as much and mostcolleges don't even require them anymore! I applied to Hampshrie collegebecause they had a lot of nontraditional students - age wise and interestwise. I'm now finishing my second year and I couldn't be happier. Thestudents don't feel like 18 tear olds fresh out of college. I am surroundedby fellow passionate learners and creators. I still had to write my 250word college essay - and I titled it "Why I am still hungry for life?"

It took a lot of courage and a lot of inertia to decide that afteryears of an "education in real life" I wanted to go through the entirecollege application process again. Then I asked myself, "If not now,when?" When I couldn't give a good enough answer, it was time to startbrowsing colleges online. Of course I thought of the practicalities. At 25,how was I going to feel surrounded by a bunch of 18-year-olds? How would Ifeel being on a campus for four years? It's been tricky making thetransition - especially since my fiancé and I just bought a house two hoursaway - but after 10 years of "real world" experience - I'm still hungryfor knowledge. I can give you more specific tips if you need them as well!

- Amy Oestreicher www.amyoes.com

When I entered college for the first time, I had completed nearly 8 years on active duty in the Air Force. At 27, I felt I was really behind those obtaining a bachelor's degree. In order to "play catch-up," I spent a lot of time with my school's counselor insuring that I was doing all the right things. This included realizing what military experience or civilian experiences I could use as credits. Because military move around frequently I wanted to insure that I took credits that could be transferred should I had to move and change schools. As I had heard of many service folks who had a ton of college credits but not enough to complete a degree in any discipline. So I completed an associate's degree using past military classes and training as electives. As luck would have it we stayed at the same base for four years enabling me to complete my bachelors.

-- Carol Gee, M.A. USAFR Retired

LAST WORD

Having a college degree certainly won't guarantee you success, because in life, there are no guarantees. But surely, having one will put in a good word for you with the right employer. It's like insurance, a back up plan, in case things go south and you find yourself standing in the unemployment line.

The beauty of going back to college is you will actually learn something. That is the point of this exercise, right? Try to not lose your sanity. Sometimes things will become too much: home responsibilities, schoolwork, and the social aspects of going to college with people half your age. Oftentimes, it'll feel like you're in secondary school. And you'd swear you didn't act like that in high school. Your high-school buddies probably did.

However, college is not right for everyone. Frankly, it was not "right" for me to go back to college as a non-traditional student. I was 10 years older and had a little more life experience to boot, though I saw it as an opportunity. I saw it as an investment in my future. I was sure that what I was doing was the right thing for me. You can also read my upcoming, yet to be released, memoir about going back to college, titled, *"Setting My Apron on Fire: Housewife Turned Undergraduate Student."* Shoot me an email to get on my mailing list, awaiting its release: sabrina.hartel@gmail.com. You can also "Like" my Facebook page: https://www.facebook.com/AreYouSureYouWantToGoBackToCollege

Are you sure you want to go back to college? Share your story.

=>> RECOMMENDED READINGS <<=

1. "90 Minute College Major Matcher." Laurence Shatkin, PH.D., Jist Publishing Inc., Indiana 2007.

2. "100 Successful College Application Essays." Second Edition. Compiled and edited by members of the staff of The Harvard Independent. New American Library, 2002.

3. "America's Top 101 Jobs for College Graduates." Sixth Edition by Michael Farr. Jist Publishing, Indiana 2005.

4. "Collins College Outlines: Basic Mathematics." Dr. Lawrence Trivieri. Harper Collins, New York 2006.

5. "Getting From College to Career: 90 Things to do Before You Join the Real World." Lindsey Pollak. Harper Collins, New York 2007.

6. "Painless Grammar." Rebecca Elliott, Ph.D. Barron's Educational Series, Inc., 1997.

7. "Real College Essays That Work." Edward B. Fiske & Bruce G. Hammond. Sourcebooks, Inc. 2006.

8. "They Don't Teach Corporate in College: A Twenty-Something's Guide to the Business World." Alexandra Levit. Career Press, New Jersey 2004.

9. "Women and Money: Owning the Power to Control Your Destiny." Suze Orman. Random House, Incorporated, 2007.

[i] Stafford, Susan H. Community College: Is it Right for You? (21) Hoboken, NJ: Wiley Publishing, Inc. 2006.

[ii] Cohen, Patricia. "Debate on Ending SAT Gains Ground." The New York Times 19 Sept. 2007: Education.

[iii] Glater, Jonathan D. "Certain Degrees Now Cost More at Public Universities." The New York Times 29 July 2007: Education.

[iv] Finder, Alan. "College Ratings Race Roars on Despite Concerns." The New York Times 17 Aug. 2007.

[v] Arenson, Karen W. "Manhattan: Noose Found at Columbia." New York Times. 10 October 2007: Education.

REFERENCES

[vi] Immerwahr, John. Foleno, Tony. "Great Expectations: How the Public and Parents—White, African-American and Hispanic View Higher Education." National Center for Public Policy and Higher Education, Public Agenda, Consortium for Policy Research in Education, National Center for Postsecondary Improvement. May 2000.

[vii] Gladieux, Lawrence. Perna, Laura. "Borrowers Who Drop Out: A Neglected Aspect of the College Student Loan Trend." National Center Report 05-2. The National Center for Public Policy and Higher Education. May 2005.

[viii] Cohen, Patricia. "Freud is Widely Taught at Universities, except in the Psychology Department." The New York Times 25 Nov. 2007: Education.

[ix] Glater, Jonathan D. "Training Law Students for Real-life Careers." The New York Times. 31 Oct. 2007.

[x] Smith, Robert M. and Associates. Learning to Learn Across the Life Span. (30-31) California: Jossey-Bass Publishers, 1990.

[xi] Smith, Robert M. and Associates. Learning to Learn Across the Life Span. (21) California: Jossey-Bass Publishers, 1990.

[xii] Smith, Robert M. and Associates. Learning to Learn Across the Life Span. (223) California: Jossey-Bass Publishers, 1990.

[xiii] Levy, Anne C. & Paludi, Michele A. Workplace Sexual Harassment. (62-63) New Jersey: Prentice-Hall, Inc. 1997.

[xiv] Table 172. Total fall enrollment in degree-granting institutions, by attendance status, age, and sex: Selected years, 1970 through 2014 – U.S. Dept. of Education, National Center for Education Statistics, Higher Education General Information Survey (HEGIS).

[xv] U.S. Equal Employment Opportunity Commission.

CPSIA information can be obtained at www.ICGtesting.com
Printed in the USA
LVOW10s1705040316

477823LV00009B/165/P